CONTEMPORARY WRITERS

General Editors
MALCOLM BRADBURY
and
CHRISTOPHER BIGSBY

DONALD BARTHELME

IN THE SAME SERIES

DONALD
BARTHELME

MAURICE COUTURIER
and
REGIS DURAND

METHUEN
LONDON AND NEW YORK

First published in 1982 by
Methuen & Co. Ltd
11 New Fetter Lane, London EC4P 4EE
Published in the USA by
Methuen & Co.
in association with Methuen, Inc.
733 Third Avenue, New York, NY 10017

Typeset by Rowland Phototypesetting Ltd
Printed in Great Britain by
Richard Clay (The Chaucer Press) Ltd
Bungay, Suffolk

British Library Cataloguing in Publication Data

Couturier, Maurice
Donald Barthelme. – (Contemporary writers)
1. Barthelme, Donald – criticism and interpretation
I. Title   II. Durand, Régis
III. Series
813'.54   PS3552.A76

ISBN 0-416-31870-3

Library of Congress Cataloging in Publication Data

Couturier, Maurice, 1939–
Donald Barthelme.
(Contemporary writers)
Bibliography: p.
1. Barthelme, Donald – Criticism and interpretation
I. Durand, Régis.   II. Title.   III. Series.
PS3552.A76Z64   1982   813'.54   82-12488
ISBN 0-416-31870-3 (pbk.)

CONTENTS

GENERAL EDITORS' PREFACE

Over the past twenty years or so, it has become clear that a decisive change has taken place in the spirit and character of contemporary writing. There now exists around us, in fiction, drama and poetry, a major achievement which belongs to our experience, our doubts and uncertainties, our ways of perceiving – an achievement stylistically radical and novel, and likely to be regarded as quite as exciting, important and innovative as that of any previous period. This is a consciousness and a confidence that has grown very slowly. In the 1950s it seemed that, somewhere amidst the dark realities of the Second World War, the great modernist impulse of the early years of this century had exhausted itself, and that the post-war arts would be arts of recessiveness, pale imitation, relative sterility. Some, indeed, doubted the ability of literature to survive the experiences of holocaust. A few major figures seemed to exist, but not a style or a direction. By the 1960s the confidence was greater, the sense of an avant-garde returned, the talents multiplied, and there was a growing hunger to define the appropriate styles, tendencies and forms of a new time. And by the 1970s it was not hard to see that we were now surrounded by a remarkable, plural, innovative generation, indeed several layers of generations, whose works represented a radical inquiry into contemporary forms and required us to read and understand – or, often, to read and *not* understand – in quite new ways. Today, as the 1980s start, that cumulative post-war achievement has acquired a degree of coherence that allows for critical response and understanding; hence the present series.

We thus start it in the conviction that the age of Beckett, Borges, Nabokov, Bellow, Pynchon, Robbe-Grillet, Golding,

Murdoch, Fowles, Grass, Handke and Calvino, of Albee, Mamet, Shepard, Ionesco, Orton, Pinter and Stoppard, of Ginsberg, Lowell, Ashbery, Paz, Larkin and Hughes, and many another, is indeed an outstanding age of international creation, striking experiment, and some degree of aesthetic coherence. It is a time that has been described as 'post-modern', in the sense that it is an era consequent to modernism yet different from it, having its own distinctive preoccupations and stylistic choices. That term has its limitations, because it is apt to generate too precise definitions of the contemporary experiment, and has acquired rather too specific associations with contemporary American writing; but it does help concentrate our sense of living in a distinctive period. With the new writing has come a new criticism or rather a new critical theorem, its thrust being 'structuralist' or 'deconstructive' – a theorem that not only coexists with but has affected that writing (to the point where many of the best theorists write fictions, the best fictionalists write criticism). Again, its theory can be hermetic and enclosing, if not profoundly apocalyptic; but it points to the presence in our time of a new sense of the status of word and text, author and reader, which shapes and structures the making of modern form.

The aim of 'Contemporary Writers' is to consider some of the most important figures in this scene, looking from the standpoint of and at the achievement of the writers themselves. Its aims are eclectic, and it will follow no tight definition of the contemporary; it will function on the assumption that contemporary writing is by its nature multidirectional and elusive, since styles and directions keep constantly changing in writers who, unlike the writers of the past, are continuous, incomplete, not dead (though several of these studies will address the careers of those who, though dead, remain our contemporaries, as many of those who continue to write are manifestly not). A fair criticism of living writers must be assertive but also provisional, just as a fair sense of contemporary style must be open to that most crucial of contemporary awarenesses, that of the suddenness of change. We do not assume, then, that there is one right path to contemporary experiment, nor that a self-conscious reflexiveness, a deconstructive strategy, an art of performance or a metafictional mode is the only one of current importance. As Iris Murdoch said, 'a strong agile realism which is of course not photographic naturalism' – associated perhaps especially with British writing, but also with Latin-American and American — is also a major component of modern style.

So in this series we wish to identify major writers, some of whom are avant-garde, others who are familiar, even popular, but all of whom are in some serious sense contemporary and in some contemporary sense serious. The aim is to offer brief, lucid studies of their work which draw on modern theoretical issues but respond, as much modern criticism does not, to their distinctiveness and individual interest. We have looked for contributors who are engaged with their subjects — some of them being significant practising authors themselves, writing out of creative experience, others of whom are critics whose interest is personal as well as theoretical. Each volume will provide a thorough account of the author's work so far, a solid bibliography, a personal judgement — and, we hope, an enlarged understanding of writers who are important, not only because of the individual force of their work, but because they are ours in ways no past writer could really be.

Norwich, England, 1981   MALCOLM BRADBURY
                                            CHRISTOPHER BIGSBY

PREFACE AND
ACKNOWLEDGEMENTS

Endings are elusive, middles are nowhere to be found, but
worst of all is to begin, to begin, to begin. (Donald Barthelme, 'The Dolt', in *Unspeakable Practices, Unnatural Acts*)

For many readers interested in the experiments of modern
fiction, Donald Barthelme is the great example of American
new fictional inquiry. It may therefore come as a surprise that
he does not particularly fancy 'metafiction', either as a word or
as a fictional mode – as he recently confessed in an interview.[1]
Yet the opening quotation here is lifted from one of his fictions
which *is* blatantly metafictional, for it narrates a man's abort-
ive attempts to compose a story: a not uncommon theme with
Barthelme. And it is not even this character, Edgar, who makes
the anxious, bored comment; it is rather the narrator or writer
himself who appears to be lamenting his fate. Yet, in the process, a story is actually told, of a sadistic baron who wants to
expose, or get rid of, his wife and her lover by using an extravagant device which will also cause thousands of deaths. Meanwhile, in the dialogue between the unsuccessful storyteller
and his patronizing wife, another tale of marital animosity
gradually emerges. As this elaborate structure testifies, Barthelme is not one of those talentless individuals who complacent-
ly parade their inability to write new stories in circuitous and
often mediocre metafictions. On the contrary, he always seems
to have *too* many stories to tell, smuggling two or three
different ones under the spurious screen of a bloated meta-
discourse, impairing his reader's ability to get things in focus.

Donald Barthelme, born in 1933 in Philadelphia, brought up
in Texas, for a time a museum director and editor of a magazine

of art and literature in New York, is a writer close to the complex evolution of contemporary art and writing. Much of his work has appeared in *The New Yorker*, and the critic can only envy those readers who stumble on his gems and unreservedly indulge in a *lecture de plaisir*, as Roland Barthes would have phrased it. For, when it comes to performing a *lecture de jouissance*, developing a critical discourse of some kind, the critic's embarrassment and difficulties are considerable. How can anyone write cogently about such ambiguous, non-linear, cacophonous fictions, complex art-objects? Every new attempt threatens to sound like the uninspired metafiction of an unimaginative hack writer. Faced with this embarrassment, we decided to focus our attention upon the embarrassment Barthelme induces in all his readers. Instead of trying to understand the author's 'purpose', or his unconscious motivations, we deliberately set out to investigate the uncanny effects his fictions produce. Until a century ago readers found it comparatively easy to identify the voice that sustained and authenticated a story. As critics, they also felt encouraged to emulate that voice in their critical discourse. Barthelme's fragmented fictions render this no longer possible. This does not prevent readers from endeavouring to synthesize a voice and reconstruct a discourse with the bits and pieces they can salvage from the text. But it will not be long before they realize that this synthetic voice sounds very much like their own.

One of the central tactics of Barthelme's fiction is the dialogue of two conspiring speakers, the self questioning and answering itself. We have constructed our study of him in a not dissimilar way. Working together and separately, we aimed to pursue both a measure of unity and a multiple impression, criticism as dialogue. Our first chapter (by MC) looks at Barthelme's word-games, and the way they serve not only to beguile the reader but to fire his intelligence and imagination. Our second (RD) dissects his humour and above all his irony in terms of displacement, rather than in the light of its social or psychological import. The third (RD) examines the way his fictions are not plausible discourses of stable subjects or narrators. The fourth (RD) looks at the modicum of communication between author and reader that remains within his unstable symbolic systems. The fifth (MC) returns Barthelme to the art gallery, looking at the sophisticated process of his vivid and often surrealistic image-making. The final chapter (MC) goes further into his artistic strategies, comparing their effects with the paradoxical, self-referential inventions of the painter Escher. Our argument is a speculation, not a *mode d'emploi*. It may just be another example of meta-criticism – a desperate attempt to exorcize the malaise every writer is subject to when starting a new text, rather than a proper beginning. But the critical record is still thin; endings are indeed elusive, middles are nowhere to be found, but worst of all is to begin, to begin, to begin . . .

The authors and publisher would like to thank the following for permission to reproduce copyright material: From *Unspeakable Practices, Unnatural Acts* by Donald Barthelme; copyright © 1964, 1965, 1966, 1967, 1968 by Donald Barthelme. From *City Life* by Donald Barthelme; copyright © 1968, 1969, 1970 by Donald Barthelme. Many of the stories contained in these collections were first published in *The New Yorker*. Reprinted by permission of Farrar, Straus & Giroux, Inc. and Deborah Rogers Ltd.

Nice and Paris, 1982   MAURICE COUTURIER
                                      REGIS DURAND

A NOTE ON THE TEXTS

Quotations from Donald Barthelme's works are taken from the first American editions, which are listed in the Bibliography. The following abbreviations have been used:

A	*Amateurs*
CBDC	*Come Back, Dr Caligari*
CL	*City Life*
DF	*The Dead Father*
GD	*Great Days*
GP	*Guilty Pleasures*
S	*Sadness*
SW	*Snow White*
UPUA	*Unspeakable Practices, Unnatural Acts*

1

DONALD BARTHELME
IN THE
LABORATORY OF DISCOURSE

Ever since the first stirrings of modern fiction, the language of novels has been an object of fascination. Up until the beginning of the twentieth century, it was generally taken for granted, however, that verbal tricksters like Tristram in *Tristram Shandy*, or even the Marcel of Proust's *The Remembrance of Things Past*, belonged, despite their amazing virtuosity, to our own 'universe of discourse' – a phrase that Donald Barthelme has playfully lifted from French structuralist jargon and put firmly before us in his novel *Snow White* (*SW*, p. 44). The modern novel can indeed be considered as a laboratory of discourse;[2] what basically distinguishes it from older romance is the fact that the telling is as important as, and often transcends, the story told – as it does in Joyce's *Ulysses*. The narrator is not now the anonymous scribe who commits to paper a well-known tale; he is an active, clever puppeteer who hides in the wings and often appears on stage to play a part of his own. Ricardou's famous aphorism about the French New Novel being essentially 'not the writing of a story but the story of a writing' could be applied, more or less adequately as the case may be, to most of the great novels and fictions written since Cervantes. In twentieth-century fiction we have seen a massive intensification of this emphasis, above all in the great experimental works like *Finnegans Wake*. And today our writers are taking it even further.

Thus what is clearly new in post-modernist fiction – this would naturally include the French New Novelists like Alain Robbe-Grillet, Claude Simon and Philippe Sollers – is that the novel's language is no longer used to simulate a plausible discourse, however elaborate or witty, but blatantly subverts the communication code. In Alain Robbe-Grillet's *Jealousy* (1957), for example, the jealous husband is not really telling his own version of a 'story' but randomly shooting a series of sequences with his own portable camera (his eyes), and playing them in haphazard order inside his private studio (his imagination). The text does not read as a transcribed discourse; it is rather a hotchpotch of recorded perceptions and images developing according to their own laws. The short and fragmented fictions of Donald Barthelme clearly belong to this same category. Even when they seem to borrow various forms of established discourses, as they constantly do, they exist only by reference and cannot be read as coherent. In the story 'The Explanation', in *City Life* (1970), for example, the following exchange gives an extraordinary twist to the sequence of questions and answers from which the narrative is made:

Q: Are you bored with the question-and-answer form?
A: I am bored with it but I realize that it permits many valuable omissions: what kind of day it is, what I'm wearing, what I'm thinking. (*CL*, p. 80)

Here and elsewhere, Barthelme is making fun of the modern tendency to bracket our discourse, to build up a meta-discourse in which the theory itself seems to take precedence over the personal involvement of the speaker. He is also stressing his own chosen omissions and dissent from realism. But he is also doing a great deal more: he is composing a fiction which is so saturated with motley fragments of recognizable discourses that it eventually becomes non-discursive. Such a fiction seems to confirm Roland Barthes's theory that first-person narrative may turn out to be the most impersonal or non-discursive form that a writer can compose. As this dialogue testifies, once our ordinary speech is transcribed, and so divorced from the body that produced it, it begins to float in a vacuum.

One of Barthelme's most disquieting fictions in this form is another story in the same collection, 'Brain Damage', where we are confronted with a series of fragments written in the apparent first person about 'the new electric awareness'. What becomes clear, though, is that the statements cannot firmly be ascribed to the same speaker or narrator:

In the first garbage dump I found a book describing a rich new life of achievement, prosperity, and happiness. (*CL*, p. 133)

We thought about the blue flowers. (*CL*, p. 134)

A dream: I am looking at a ship, an ocean-going vessel the size of the Michelangelo. (*CL*, p. 137)

I worked for newspapers. (*CL*, p. 138)

The absence of cross-references in these fragments makes it impossible to decide whether or not it is the same 'speaker' who is uttering all these 'I's and 'we's. These fragments could be the rational utterances made on various occasions by a sane person, or a collage of statements made by a group of speakers, or the irrational utterances made at some particular time by a madman. The last interpretation seems the most logical, since the fiction is apparently about madness. But there is another that is probably more appealing: Barthelme is not attempting to simulate a plausible discourse, however crazy, but trying to confuse the reader's mind and make him feel what it is like to be suffering, in that new electric awareness, from 'brain damage'.

Certainly, as we read through Barthelme's stories, novels and visual collages, we have the uncanny feeling that someone is showing us around a lunatic asylum to test our sanity, introducing us to megalomaniac inmates who take themselves to be figures like Paul Klee, General Kellerman or the President of the United States. Each individual character we come across may brazenly assert his ego without a shadow of doubt as to his real identity; but identities in words readily dissolve, as they do with the notional 'Robert Kennedy' in 'Robert Kennedy Saved from Drowning', in *Unspeakable Practices, Unnatural Acts* (1968). The sane visitor, whom the reader presumably considers himself to be, does not feel like arguing with these people for fear of precipitating a storm in their tormented brains, or may indeed feel afraid of being contaminated if he gets too involved in their arcane worlds. He is in much the position as K. in Kafka's *The Castle*, who was not at first aware of having landed in another 'universe of discourse', and vainly tried to argue with the people around him, while not realizing that they did not rely on the same presuppositions and representations as he did. Barthelme's reader is similarly unable to enjoy the privileges he has taken for granted in reading fiction: Olympian aloofness, a patronizing condescension toward the characters and narrators. He is utterly seduced by an absolute freedom of speech apparently shared by all the would-be narrators and characters, and by the constant flouting of the linguistic code. At the same time, however, he tends to lose countenance when he realizes that something has been wrenched from him by underhand means he neither masters nor even understands. As the philosopher Jean Baudrillard keeps repeating in a recent book, there is always a price to be paid for seduction – acquiescence and surrender.[3]

So the casual – as well as the serious – reader of Barthelme spontaneously senses that he is not considered a qualified or trustworthy interlocutor of either the multifaceted narrators of these works or the secretive author who creates them. He has the disturbing impression that this inaccessible individual is writing for his own perverse or guilty pleasures and is not taking his audience into account. The ominiscient author of more conventional fiction, on the other hand, is always very much aware of his audience and the referential compacts he makes with it – as Barthelme keeps reminding us in his allusions to the fictions of previous realism. Thus, as he puts it in 'Engineer-Private Paul Klee Misplaces an Aircraft between Milbertshofen and Cambrai, March 1916', in *Sadness* (1972): 'with omniscience and omnipresence, hand-in-hand as it were, goes omnipotence. . . . We yearn to be known, acknowledged, admired even' (*S*, p. 66). The godlike narrator whom Sartre ridiculed was no more than a conventional disguise in which the timorous author wrapped his devouring pride. Certainly this narrative strategy allowed a high level of exchange between author and reader. With Barthelme, no such communication is established: each narrator (one wonders if the word means anything any more) is imprisoned in his private 'universe of discourse' and does not seem to acknowledge, however obliquely, the actual or future presence of an audience.

The reader's embarrassment is even worse, of course, when the fiction he reads includes pictures. In 'At the Tolstoy Museum' (*CL*) or 'The Flight of Pigeons from the Palace' (*S*), for instance, we find a narrative or descriptive text, plus drawings or photographs, plus block-letter captions which often have little to do with the pictures. The collage technique, which Barthelme practised with considerable success until *Sadness*, was not, of course, new, but perhaps it had never been exploited so efficiently in short fictions where the reader spontaneously looks for a sustained discourse or a linear narrative. A surrealist painting based on the same technique is puzzling

16

too, but we tend not to worry about the sanity of the artist. Where language is concerned, however, we feel that no one can tamper with it like this and claim to be in their right mind, because we usually consider that a good mastery of language is the best proof anyone can give of their sanity. This technique – which includes not only the mixing of text and pictures but also the listing of questions ('Kierkegaard Unfair to Schlegel', 'Concerning the Bodyguard') or of unrelated statements ('The Explanation', *The Dead Father*), or the evocation of miscellaneous topics ('What to do Next') – makes it impossible for the reader to decide what the story is about, simply because no single speaker can be identified. All these devices stagger our imagination, baffle our intelligence, and eventually induce us to evolve our private interpretation, no matter how extravagant it may be, to escape the tension and embarrassment.

In *Pale Fire* (1962), Vladimir Nabokov had inaugurated this brain-testing form of fiction on a large scale: he created two different discourses, that of Shade, the poet, and that of Kinbote, the commentator, and two or even three diverging narratives – the biography of Shade, the history of the King of Zembla, the history of the poem. The question that still perplexes the critics can be stated in terms borrowed from Humpty-Dumpty: 'Which is to be master?' Which, of Shade or Kinbote, can satisfy the reader that he is the prime or the sole narrator of this puzzling book? We take too easily for granted that people speak or write mostly to give a coherent view of themselves, to show that they enjoy a satisfactory understanding of, or power over, the world they live in. Of course, the Nabokov aficionado is aware that the problem of motivations is irrelevant, that it is raised by the reader when he is puzzled with a book and can make no sense of it. What Nabokov and Barthelme are probably both inviting us to do is to change our outlook altogether, to take possession of their texts boldly and without inhibitions – in other words, to read them creatively.

It was Joyce, of course, who first took the tremendous risk of overriding the principle of narrative coherence dramatically. But, whereas the delirious language of *Finnegans Wake* could conceivably be located as the senseless logorrhoea of a demented scholar, the disrupted and often abstract language of Barthelme's fictions seems to have no such referential anchorings, however questionable they may be. When these short fictions appeared in periodicals, they looked strange, of course, but not half as baffling as they are now in their respective collections. We usually consider that there are limits to the number and variety of discourses a given speaker or writer can imitate or invent, to the variety of subjects he can tackle, to the wealth of objects he can create. In this case, we definitely feel that these limits have been transgressed, and we find it difficult to conceive of the insane or talented word-handler who has shattered them. Many critics have taken Barthelme to task for his incapacity to write long fictions. It is true that both his novels – *Snow White* (1967) and *The Dead Father* (1976) – look very much like collections of short fictions, except for the fact that the same characters turn up in the various sequences. But this may be his individual achievement too: he has proved capable of creating (and not simply pastiching or simulating) countless discourses which do not seem to reflect the workings of an individual mind or unconscious but rather a great variety of both. Each fiction seems to be an *objet trouvé*, the senseless utterance of an anonymous (and improbable) speaker (*GD*, p. 71), like 'Question Party', which Barthelme says he lifted from *Godey's Lady's Book* (the popular monthly published in Philadelphia between 1830 and 1898).

This obsessional search, on the part of the reader, for an identifiable and stable discourse is somewhat morbid, of course; but, ever since Henry James, Percy Lubbock and E. M. Forster, critics who have worked on fiction have been unable to avoid being caught in it. Apparently it is difficult to accept Borges' theory that literary works are the product and out-growth of other books written before them. A defiant novelist like Nabokov, for instance, could not consent to the idea that each individual writer's contribution to the 'Library of Babel' was only slight. In our Western world, where every human being is considered to be a valuable entity endowed with both freedom and the capacity to create, individual achievements have always drawn respect and admiration, as the prestige of the Prometheus myth testifies. The contribution of Marxist criticism, on the other hand, has no doubt been to show that a literary work is as much the product of a language, a literary tradition and a national history as the personal accomplish-ment of the individual writer – though, at times, this type of criticism overshoots the mark and tends to underplay the personal achievement of the artist.

Barthelme's approach to the problem of literary discourse is neither that of the Marxists nor that of Borges. His Snow White may express his view on the subject when she says: 'Oh I wish there were some words in the world that were not the words I always hear!' (*SW*, p. 6). He seems at times to be dreaming of developing a new language as he writes, of doing without the well-worn language of his cultural community. This new language would be something like the ultimate non-discourse that Joyce sought to create in *Finnegans Wake*. Although Barthelme is probably aware that this dream can never be fulfilled, during the last twenty years he has worked hard to stretch the capacities of the English language. And he has succeeded, to a certain extent, in evolving an idiom all his own.

*

This idiom is characterized in the first place by its high degree of impersonality. The number and peculiarity of the passive sentences, for instance, are quite amazing in his fictions – as we see, for example, in the following passage from 'Brain Damage': 'At the restaurant, sadness was expressed. Black napkins were draped over black arms. Black table-cloths were distributed. Several nearby streets were painted black' (*CL*, p. 136). This passage reads a little like the sentence from *Snow White*: 'the loss of equanimity was serious' (*SW*, p. 112). Barthelme seems like an arch-materialist in comparison with the inhabitants of Borges' Tlön, whose world is made not of objects but of independent acts, as the absence of nouns in their language testifies; Barthelme, on the other hand, uses abstract nouns to describe the mood of his characters. 'Sadness' and 'equanimity' appear to refer to essences which the characters accidentally happen to run across. Man is like a chance visitor in a world teeming with universals. The passive form is the archetypal structure in this new language, on that other planet: it transmutes the fundamental elements in the sentence, so that the subject now expresses the accidental ('sadness', 'loss of equanimity'), and the predicate ('was expressed', 'was serious') erases the existential subject.

Barthelme has presented a similar kind of metaphysical displacement in 'Sentence', a fiction made of one single sentence which deals with the process of writing a sentence. Here is the beginning:

Or a long sentence moving at a certain pace down the page

19

aiming for the bottom – if not the bottom of this page then of some other page – where it can rest, or stop for a moment to think about the questions raised by its own (temporary) existence . . . (*CL*, p. 107)

The problem of the existence, however temporary, of a sentence is not usually considered of such metaphysical importance, and hardly makes a fitting subject for a fiction. On the other hand, we constantly invent new sentences to evoke and reinforce the existence of what we take to be real objects or imaginary representations. What happens, then, when a sentence merely promotes its own existence? This is one of the mind-boggling questions that Hofstadter tries to answer in his excellent book *Gödel, Escher, Bach* (1980). In fact, it is impossible to distinguish the sentence *qua* fiction from the fiction *qua* sentence, or the primary discourse from the meta-discourse (the discourse which builds up the fiction from the discourse upon the discourse which unfolds the story which is itself about writing a sentence!). A similar effect is produced by Escher's lithograph *Drawing Hands*, in which two hands are reciprocally drawing each other. In both the fiction and the lithograph, we are fascinated by this circularity; we are caught in the vicious circle and tend to forget the artists who produced such extraordinary works. In other words, we cease to be concerned with the discourse and let ourselves become engrossed in the confusing complexity of the objects.

Barthelme, then, like Escher, manages to divert our attention from himself by drawing it towards the technical feats. When we read his fictions, we tend to feel as if we were reading the works of a gifted and imaginative linguist who has invented brilliant examples to illustrate his theories. Unlike other innovative writers, he has created comparatively few words: 'horsewife' for 'housewife' (*SW*, p. 99), 'copted out' for 'opted/copped out' (*SW*, p. 139), 'hurlment' (*SW*, p. 159), 'vatricide' (*SW*, p. 164). On the other hand, he has metamorphosed common words by combining them in very strange pairs like 'more dead' (*DF*, p. 74), a phrase that violates a semantic rule (a comparative form can be used only with gradable adjectives). Some of his best stylistic strokes similarly sound like samples specially tailored to illustrate a linguistic law. In 'The Balloon', for instance, the acceptability of the word 'sullied' is tested in the following way: 'One man might consider that the balloon had to do with the notion *sullied*, as in the sentence *The big balloon sullied the otherwise clear and radiant Manhattan sky*' (*UPUA*, p. 18). This man, like most of Barthelme's characters, is highly intellectual: he does not pick up words at random, as most people do in everyday life, but ratiocinates and procrastinates, as if reality did not constrain him to react to the force of circumstances.

In fact, the characters seem less concerned with adjusting themselves to a given situation than with conforming their several discourses to, or parading their perfect mastery of, the linguistic code. In *Snow White*, when Henry asks what an interrupted screw is, Dan, instead of stating the obvious, offers the following definition:

> 'An interrupted screw . . . is a screw with a discontinuous helix, as in a cannon breech, formed by cutting away part or parts of the thread, and sometimes part of the shaft. Used with a lock nut having corresponding male sections.' 'This filthy,' Henry said . . . (*SW*, pp. 29–30)

Henry, like most people, is less interested in such metalinguistic statements than in plain sexual experience. This elaborate definition, crammed with sexually loaded words, does sound filthy; but it also provides a good metaphorical description of the real thing. Barthelme is here using words as performing puppets or monkeys, forcing the reader to rediscover the ambiguity of the phrase 'interrupted screw' and to realize that the most common metaphor used in technical jargon is probably the sexual one. Conversely, when the serious linguist playfully tests the verb 'to come', he manages to stay away from the sexual meaning: 'We learn to make sentences. Come to me. May I come to your house? Christmas comes but once a year. I'll come to your question. The light comes and goes' (*DF*, p. 16). By deliberately refusing to use the word as a synonym for 'to have an orgasm', Barthelme succeeds in highlighting the extraordinary ambiguity of this word. What he is suggesting, apparently, is that, whenever we use a word in a restricted sense, we cannot blot out all its other meanings, whether or not they occur to us.

This poetic testing of language does not stop at the lexical level but extends also to the semantic. At times we are reminded of Chomsky's well-known example: 'Colorless green ideas sleep furiously.' With Barthelme, the laws regulating the pairing of words ('selection restrictions', in linguistic parlance) seem to have been abolished, as we see in the following passage: '"You're supposed to be curing a ham." "The ham died," she said. "I couldn't cure it"' ('The Piano Player', *CBDC*, p. 19). There is nothing wrong with 'curing a ham', where 'cure' means 'to subject to a preservative process'. On the other hand, the sentence 'The ham died' is clearly unacceptable: only live things can be said to die. Here, as in the case of the 'interrupted screw', Barthelme is forcing us to hold in our minds two mutually exclusive meanings of the same word. The problem assumes metaphysical proportions when we realize that a ham cannot be cured in the sense of 'to heal' because it is not a live thing, but that it once was part of a live animal (now past curing) and as such requires 'curing' if it must be preserved. We find similar violations of semantic rules in 'a troupe of agoutis performed tax evasion atop tall, swaying yellow poles', or in 'We auditioned an explosion' ('The Flight of Pigeons from the Palace', *S*, pp. 132, 134). These verbal feats, which, as we shall see in Chapter 5, produce striking images, compel us to do some amount of linguistic investigation to discover what is amiss, and thereby draw the attention to themselves and away from the discourse.

These acts of linguistic vandalism are, of course, not as innocent as they may seem. They contribute to changing our representation of reality in a drastic way. Consider, for example, the following utterance: 'The world is sagging, snagging, scaling, spalling, pilling, pinging, pitting, warping, checking, fading, chipping, cracking, yellowing, leaking, staling, shrinking, and in dynamic unbalance' ('Down the Line with the Annual', *GP*, p. 6). This is not only a 'constative statement', as John Austin would have phrased it. Barthelme does not simply portray a changing world; he also helps to change it in his own way by assaulting it with multiple words and unheard-of phrases. He gives the impression that reality has lost its power to force words upon him and his characters, that language is at last free from it and constitutes a private world where everything is possible at any moment.

This process may be the one described as 'the disenchantment of symbols' in the following fragment from 'The Glass Mountain': '97. I approached the symbol, with its layers of meaning, but when I touched it, it changed into a beautiful princess' (*CL*, pp. 64–5). In our modern world, where a multiplicity of learned discourses force us to see the 'layers of meaning' that cover any trivial phenomenon or object, we have become unable to look at the world naïvely, or, as Ernst Cassirer would have put it, 'iconically'. From what has been said so far, it might seem that Barthelme is largely serving to multiply the number of layers; in fact, the prime lesson that can be drawn from this linguistic analysis, which emulates Barthelme's own research, is that language has a life of its own which no amount of scientific investigation can ever hope to describe or comprehend. This parodic process of interpretative exhaustion, in which all these fictions seem to be involved, baffles our intellect and cleanses our imagination and our senses of the obstructing grids (scientific, philosophical or otherwise). Whereas traditional fiction tried to study the functionings of human discourse and to evolve intellectual statements about the products of intuition, perception and imagination, this kind of fiction strives to reverse the trend: its appealing nonsense, which flouts all our learned discourses, cannot be reduced to tame structures. We need a new, enlarged form of intelligence to appreciate it, an intelligence that will tap the resources of the senses and the imagination. We must discipline ourselves into considering literary works as basically non-discursive (as Derrida already invited us to do in *De la grammatologie*[4]), in order fully to appreciate their iconicity.

2

BARTHELME'S
ART OF DISPLACEMENT

To read Barthelme's works is to experience the power and strangeness of fragmentation. 'Fragments are the only form I trust': this phrase in 'See the Moon?' (*UPUA*, p. 153) is one of his most frequently quoted, though it is seldom made clear that it is not spoken by the writer but by one of his narrators. Starting from there, it is certainly possible to carry the game further and piece together from his occasional remarks a kind of patchy aesthetic manifesto. From the same collection, there would then be the narrator who expresses anguish at the thought of linearity and rational construction: 'Thinking of anything was beyond him. I sympathize. I myself have these problems. Endings are elusive, middles are nowhere to be found, but worst of all is to begin, to begin, to begin' ('The Dolt', *UPUA*, p. 65). Or there are the claims of a tragicomic fear of uttering words, the fear of excretion which is barely counterbalanced by the security that the single word affords:

> 'Some people', Miss R. said, 'run to conceits or wisdom but I hold to the hard, brown, nutlike word. I might point out that there is enough aesthetic excitement here to satisfy anyone but a damned fool.' ('The Indian Uprising', *UPUA*, p. 9)

One could indeed amass a string of such useful remarks and, if it would not amount to much of an aesthetic theory, it would at least spell out the distrust of language, the difficulty of articulation, the dislocation of coherence and the displaced sense of nostalgia for continuous forms that run through his work. Fragments may be the only form some of the characters trust; but is it not for want of a whole and, who knows, even of a *meaning*? This is what the narrator who 'trusts only fragments' exclaims:

> It's my hope that these . . . souvenirs . . . will someday merge, blur – cohere is the word, maybe – into something meaningful. A grand word, meaningful. What do I look for? A work of art, I'll not accept anything less. Yes I know it's shatteringly ingenuous but I wanted to be a painter. ('See the Moon?', *UPUA*, p. 152)

But of course there is the possibility that this (like the remark on fragments) is disingenuously ironic, or consciously uttered in self-pity, or simply thrown in as a red herring for critics. Clearly, those explicit statements culled from the texts cannot be trusted. It is in the writing itself that the power of fragmentation is experienced by the reader. It is experienced primarily, of course, at the level of narrative. We have indeed been trained as readers to expect and to value narrative as the foremost component of the pleasure of reading fiction (dialogue is another, to a lesser degree, but only so long as it is framed and structured by a narrative – which is precisely what is missing from Barthelme's recent dialogue pieces, as we shall see later). But fragmentation goes well beyond the simple disruption of narrative codes. It is not just a technique or a gimmick – or, if it is, its effectiveness is limited. It is a mode of apprehending the world and the concept; it is a process, not a formula (which explains why it is preferable to speak of *fragmentation* rather than of fragments). Maurice Blanchot has splendidly commented on the painful and paradoxical nature of fragmentation:

> To speak of the fragment must not be solely in reference to the fragmentation of an already existing reality, nor to a moment of a totality which is to come. This is difficult to consider because of the exigency of our comprehension, according to which there can only be a knowledge of the whole, just as a view is always comprehensive; according to this comprehension, there should be, where there is a fragment, an implicit designation of something whole, whether it was so previously or whether it is going to become so in the future – the cut-off finger refers to the hand, just as the first atom prefigures the universe and contains it within itself. Our thinking is thus caught between two limits, the imagina-

tion of substantial integrity, and the imagination of dialectical evolution.[5]

In Barthelme's stories, there is almost always 'a playful disruption of our accepted forms of discourse and understanding'.[6] But his concern is not merely (not even perhaps primarily) with *forms*; rather it is with the interaction between the real (its signs and its meaning) and the self (its imaginative power and its emotions). Form is the result of this interface, language the best index to it, the very locus of the tensions, the disorder, the entropy that result. Barthelme's references to language as waste, *dreck*, to the 'trash phenomenon', are well known. Often, as in *Snow White*, his strategy is to turn the condition to an advantage, to make a comedy of it with a kind of 'camp' aesthetic enjoyment:

> We like books that have a lot of *dreck* in them, matter which presents itself as not wholly relevant (or indeed, at all relevant) but which, carefully attended to, can supply a kind of 'sense' of what is going on. This 'sense' is not to be obtained by reading between the lines (for there is nothing there, in those white spaces), but by reading the lines themselves – looking at them, and so arriving at a feeling not of satisfaction exactly, that is too much to expect, but of having read them; of having 'completed' them. (*SW*, p. 106)

Clichés, tags, scraps of everyday conversations, old quotes, are reassuring because of their low degree of activity, because of their inertia. But, whenever you speak, there is a danger that something will start vibrating frantically, will slip off your tongue, run amok: '"There are worms in words" the general cries, "the worms in words are, like Mexican jumping beans, agitated by the warmth of the mouth!"' ('A Picture History of the War', *UPUA*, p. 137). This proneness to Brownian agitation is inherent in the act of speech itself. And the fear of the frantic disorder and disruption that may ensue is the reason why enunciation sometimes turns into an extraordinary adventure, a painful and hazardous extraction:

> I wanted to say a certain thing to a certain man, a certain true thing that had crept into my head. I opened my head at the place provided, and proceeded to pronounce the true thing that lay languishing there – that is, proceeded to propel that

26

trueness, that felicitous trularity from its place inside my head out into world life. The certain man stood waiting to receive it. His face reflected an eager acceptingness. Everything was right: I propelled, using my mind, my mouth, all my muscles. I propelled. I propelled and propelled. I felt that trularity inside my head moving slowly through the passage provided (stained like the caves of Lascaux with garlic, antihistamines, Berlioz, a history, a history) towards its debut on the world's stage . . . ('A Picture History of the War', *UPUA*, p. 131)

This wonderful piece of linguistic comedy has affinities with the Woody Allen type of burlesque fantasy; at the same time it is not unrelated, from a psychological point of view, to the discourse of obsessive neurotics. Speech is difficult, but there are reasons for the difficulty, the ambivalent retention/excretion of the speaker. Once delivered from its cavities, its festering recesses, speech proliferates. It takes over, subverts – and the subversion causes anxiety and depression:

> What is 'wailing'? What is 'funky'? Why does language subvert me, subvert my seniority, my medals, my oldness, whenever it gets a chance? What does language have against me – me that has been good to it, respecting its little peculiarities and nicilosities, for sixty years. (*UPUA*, p. 130)

Once free, language is tentacular, predatory; it ensnares and dissolves. Every utterance is an aggression, a cannibalistic dispossession: 'The moment I inject discourse from my universe of discourse (u. of d.) into your u. of d., the yourness of yours is diluted' (*SW*, p. 46). Hence the reassuring quality of *dreck*. Hence also the satisfaction in the minimal achievement outlined above: to have reached the end of a line, of a sentence, to have 'completed' them. Portrait of the artist as antisemiotician, as post-Beckettian minimalist.

You can counteract the threat of proliferation and loss of sense by clutching at little things, the flotsam and jetsam of language. But you can also, in a classical reversal, desire (or act as if you desired) the loss itself, even though it is the negation of all coherent discourse. In Swift's Academy of Lagado, the concepts (the 'signified') are lacking – which makes it necessary to turn to the things themselves (the 'referent') in order to communicate: you carry your whole vocabulary on your back.

In Barthelme's 'Paraguay', in order to face the stress of proliferation you can buy ingredients to mix with language, to thin it, with a pinch of silence – or a pinch of noise (that which does not make sense):

> In the larger stores silence (damping materials) is sold in paper sacks like cement. Similarly, the softening of language, usually lamented as a falling off from former practice, is in fact a clear response to the proliferation of surfaces and stimuli. Imprecise sentences lessen the strain of close tolerances. Silence is also available in the form of white noise. ('Paraguay', *CL*, p. 27)

Barthelme is telling us here in effect that displacement is the nature of language, not only synchronically and superficially (along the surfaces and encounters of everyday life), but also in depth, diachronically.

Every language is historical: it does not become poorer or disintegrate; it only changes with the culture. Barthelme's language is intimately bound up with contemporary American culture, and with the crises and changes that shape it. The language he writes in (and about) is a displaced idiom, an idiom of displacement. And, as with all displaced bodies, empty spaces, scars and longings are perceptible, even though there may be an attempt to conceal them behind a playful acceptance or justification (and perhaps even desire) of what is essentially unacceptable, unjustifiable – the loss of all values and points of reference. Caught in a double bind, Barthelme's language (and through him the language of the culture) is a deeply neurotic one, from which only some fragments will emerge, having escaped entropy, noise or sheer drivel: the celebrated 'fragments', of course, but also lists, repertories and catalogues: ' "The only form of discourse of which I approve", said Miss R. in her dry, tense voice, "is the litany" ' ('The Indian Uprising', *UPUA*, p. 8).

This 'theory' of language is cultural, but it is also psychological. It goes inevitably with a certain perception not only of the connections between culture and individual speech, but also of the connections between an individual and his or her own language. Barthelme's fiction, as we shall see, stages a central speaking voice or subject, with a weak sense of identity, constantly seeking refuge in fantasy, word-play or self-pity, endlessly playing games of delusion which barely conceal a terror of failure, loss and disintegration. The two aspects implied in the concept of displacement (topological as well as psychological) are perfectly in evidence here, and they come together in one essential element of Barthelme's fiction: *humour*.

*

Barthelme's comedy of language relies on many devices: puns, nonsense, slapstick, the transformation or fabrication of words (as in, for example, the very funny mock-confession in 'A Picture History of the War', *UPUA*, p. 129). He also uses repetition, improvisation, nursery rhymes, variations on a syntactic structure (pseudo-alternatives, or the use of the passive voice, as in 'The Flight of the Pigeons from the Palace', *S*). But all of those techniques can be subsumed under the single process we call humour. We take humour – or, at any rate, the structural principle of humour – to be, after the French philosopher Gilles Deleuze, 'the art of surfaces', the art of displacement itself.[7]

Freud, too, saw in humour 'a peculiar technique comparable to displacement'. The actual definition he gives in *Jokes and their Relations to the Unconscious* is rather heavily forbidding, but it does help one understand the sleight-of-hand that takes place in the process, the sudden shunting of energy from unpleasure to pleasure:

> Humour can be regarded as the highest of these defensive processes. It scorns to withdraw the ideational content bearing the distressing affect from conscious attention as repression does, and thus surmounts the automatism of defence. It brings this about by finding a means of withdrawing the energy from the release of unpleasure that is already in preparation and of transforming it, by discharge into pleasure.[8]

Freud shows elsewhere that jokes, the comic and humour all rely on a process of displacement, at different levels. In the case of jokes (*Witze*), it is a displacement of energy originally intended for inhibition, towards pleasurable expenditure; in the case of the comic, it is a displacement of energy originally intended for cathexis; finally, in the case of humour proper, it is energy reserved for affects and emotions. Beyond the purely economic definition, Gilles Deleuze offers a view of humour that brings together a rich cluster of concepts, operations and paradoxes which have a direct bearing on textuality. Foremost among them is *irony*, often described as antithetical or complementary to humour, but whose relation to it is somewhat more complex. This is best seen in a story that is apparently almost exclusively concerned with irony.

In this story, 'Kierkegaard Unfair to Schlegel', Barthelme, following Kierkegaard's analysis, shows that irony can be understood only within the framework of a romantic theory of the self, to which the opposition subject/object is essential: 'Irony is a means of depriving the object of its reality in order that the subject may feel free.' Deleuze shows that the theory of irony rests on the identity of contraries, irony being the negative force *par excellence*. Barthelme says: 'irony becomes an infinite absolute negativity'. But humour operates differently: it refuses dualities, scorns depth and height in favour of surfaces. And reading Deleuze's essay (and especially chapter 19, 'On Humour') we understand much more clearly what is at stake in Barthelme's story: nothing less than the place of contemporary discourse (or, rather, its lack of definite place, its displacement); meanwhile its subject, the interplay between fictionalists and philosophers, outlines the essentially intertextual nature of contemporary writing.

Deleuze quotes a passage from Kierkegaard which illuminates the logic of irony. Irony, too, involves displacement, but a displacement of a particular nature based on the permanence of a 'fundamental I':

> The soul that practises irony is like the soul that travels throughout the world in the doctrine of Pythagoras. It is always on the move, but it no longer needs such a long span of time. Like children at their game, the ironist counts on his fingers: rich man, poor man, beggar man, etc. All those incarnations only represent for him pure potentialities, so that he can run their gamut as fast as children playing their game. . . . If reality thus loses its value in the ironist's eyes, it is not because it has been outgrown and must make room for a more authentic reality, but because the ironist embodies the 'fundamental I' to which there is no corresponding reality.[9]

In the light of this commentary, then, Barthelme is and is not an ironist. He is, inasmuch as through various personae and

30

fictional voices and garbs he plays the game of dressing up with nimble versatility. He is not, in the sense that his constantly shifting positions are no longer linked to a 'fundamental I' but only to an endless displacement. Where irony preserves a fixed point of reference, humour describes what happens in the post-modernist text when the core vanishes. Where irony is linked to the individual ego, humour brings in the art of surfaces and duplicates, of 'nomadic singularities' (in Deleuze's phrase).

So this story offers a striking illustration of the shift from an 'ironic' to a 'humorous' attitude in post-modern American fiction. Barthelme quotes at length from Kierkegaard's *The Concept of Irony* and the supposedly 'unfair' treatment in it of Schlegel's novel *Lucinda*. Whole passages thus become pieces of intellectual *dreck* in Barthelme's 'super-fiction'. A comedy of quotations and theoretical displacements begins:

> Irony deprives the object of its reality when the ironist says something about the object that is not what he means. Kierkegaard distinguishes between the phenomenon (the word) and the essence (the thought or meaning). Truth demands an identity of essence and phenomenon. But with irony quote the phenomenon is not the essence but the opposite of the essence (unquote page 264). The object is deprived of its reality by what I have said about it. Regarded in an ironical light, the object shivers, shatters, disappears. Irony is thus destructive and what Kierkegaard worries about a lot is that irony has nothing to put in the place of what it has destroyed. The new actuality – what the ironist has said about the object – is peculiar in that it is a comment upon a former actuality rather than a new actuality. This account of Kierkegaard's account of irony is grossly over-simplified. Now, consider an irony directed not against a given object but against the whole of existence. An irony directed against the whole of existence produces, according to Kierkegaard, estrangement and poetry . . . quote irony no longer directs itself against this or that particular phenomenon, against a particular thing unquote. Quote the whole of existence has become alien to the ironic subject (unquote page 261). (*CL*, pp. 94–5)

As this comedy proceeds, twist after twist of 'irony' is being revealed, until the speaking voice turns out to be directly implicated:

Because that is not what I think at all. We have to do here with my own irony. Because of course Kierkegaard was 'fair' to Schlegel. In making a statement to the contrary I am attempting to . . . I might have several purposes – simply being provocative, for example. But mostly I am trying to annihilate Kierkegaard in order to deal with his disapproval

Q: of Schlegel?

A: of me (*CL*, pp. 96–7)

This scene, in a parody of the psychoanalytic method, shows how irony becomes a defence in the face of a danger for the subject, a subject who once again shows signs of a paranoid nature. But it also shows that the drift of Barthelme's fiction is not really towards irony as such, in spite of the splendid clown army of people and places conjured up throughout its pages. The fundamental drift in this fiction is one that involves a deprived superego, stricken by the loss of the good object: the Father in all his guises (father, dead father, psychoanalyst, etc.) – a loss and a deprivation that are incessantly, obsessively played out.

If, according to Jacques Lacan, humour is precisely 'the transference into the comic mode of the very function of the superego',[10] then this definition completes the circle for the time being. Barthelme's fiction, ruled by displacement, is a manic-depressive drama of the superego, a battle, a race in which most of the verbal artefacts of our culture are summoned up. The race is, among other things, between elation and depression, tears and laughter, anguish caused by the loss and temporary relief at finding a substitute. So this fiction goes on, by fits and starts and fragments, never at one with itself, propelled forward by its constitutive principle – its instability, the art of displacement.

3

BARTHELME AND THE ECLIPSE OF THE SUBJECT

Donald Barthelme's is an art of absences. It is absence that dominates his novel *The Dead Father* (1976), where nineteen men drag the great Dead Father – who is not entirely dead, since he speaks – to some ultimate tomb. What has gone from the world that was once there is a recurrent theme; his writings suggest a call for new emotions and understandings. And the most striking feature of all his stories – from the early work of *Come Back, Dr Caligari* (1964) to the later work of *Great Days* (1979) – is the absence of the *subject*, of a stable, confident self. This lack of confidence affects everything: language, as we have seen, but also the speaker, other people and one's own narrating self:

> Moments of self-doubt . . .
> 'Am I really a—'
> 'What does it *mean* to be a—'
> 'Can one *refuse* to be a—' ('The Genius', *S*, p. 32)

Of course, this sense of insecurity and precarious identity is tied up with discourse, with its discontinuities, hesitations and aporias. It is nowhere more clear than in Barthelme's writings that we have our symbolic being in language. Thus if, for instance, it becomes almost impossible to connect, to string sentences and narratives together, then the self is locked in anguish and panic: 'The part of the story that came next was suddenly missing, I couldn't think of it, so I went into the next room and drank a glass of water (my "and then" still hanging in the frangible air)' ('And then', *A*, p. 105).

So sequences fail; and symptoms of disfunction, such as 'sadness', melancholia and amnesia, are everywhere. Hence the

33

endless questioning that runs through his texts, eliciting meaningless answers or, more likely, no answer at all:

> Having assigned myself a task that is beyond my abilities, why do I then do that which is most certain to preclude my completing the task? To ensure failure? To excuse failure? Ordinary fear of failure?
>
> When I characterize the task as beyond my abilities, do I secretly believe that it is within my powers?
>
> Was there only one crucial error, or was there a still more serious error earlier, one that I did not recognize as such at the time?
>
> Was there a series of errors? ('The Agreement', *A*, p. 61)

Such doubts and anxieties spread to all areas of life – especially in the bleak volume *Sadness* (1972), which, as the title of the first story indicates, is a real 'critique de la vie quotidienne'. Yet self-analysis is of little or no avail; information, passion and skill may help, but only temporarily. Despite this, the situation seems to generate an energy of its own, vitality as well as depression, as in the story 'The Rise of Capitalism': 'Doubt is a necessary precondition to meaningful action. Fear is the great mover in the end' (*S*, p. 146). And it is this strange mixture of affects and effects that we must now examine more closely.

'Smoke, rain, abulia': this fiction evidently dwells in the ravaged land of what Barthelme in one story names as 'brain damage' – in the aftermath of some unidentified traumatic event, of which we may know only the symptoms, the signs: a void, a deprivation, a disaster, leaving behind a host of painful affects, like fear, guilt, anxiety and disconnection. In his work these affects seem, most of the time, to be floating – unrelated to a specific, particular situation. More like a permanent condition of the subject, they are not clearly induced by a psychological context; rather, they seem to be waiting for something to fasten on to, a situation they can take over and claim as their correspondent in the 'real' world. One repeated sign is the ubiquitous 'failure' of 'a relationship' – a dominant theme in *Amateurs* (1976), and very explicitly displayed in the last story, 'At the End of the Mechanical Age'. Thus 'brain damage' is everywhere. Like the existence of the unconscious itself, there is no running away from it; it will manifest itself all the time. All one can hope for is the occasional flicker of felicitous unconsciousness, 'skiing along the soft surface of brain damage, never to sink, because we don't understand the danger –' ('Brain Damage', *CL*, p. 156). Or to be like the wapituil – to develop the ability to lose interest very quickly, to lead a life entirely of the moment, made up of 'one of each things', to be able to conceptualize but not to follow through, to lose oneself in the reminiscence of each unique flash of experience ('The sex life of a wapituil consists of a single experience, which he thinks about for a long time', *CL*, p. 150).

To escape this condition, to find a life whole and meaningful, whatever that could be, is a meretricious dream, a quack's promise:

> In the first garbage dump I found a book describing a rich new life of achievement, prosperity, and happiness. A rich new life of achievement, prosperity and happiness could not be achieved alone, the book said. It must be achieved with the aid of *spirit teachers*. (*CL*, p. 143)

Such a vision cannot even be called a fantasy, because there does not seem to be much desire invested in it. It is as if the damage was too great, the regression too far gone. In 'Me and Miss Mandible' the protagonist, although 35 years old and fully grown-up, finds himself back in high school and 'officially a child'. Yet he is strangely compliant with the decision that has been made to 're-adjust' him, aware that he needs 'reworking in some fundamental way'. There is no sense, in him, of an individual self whose integrity is being tampered with, only a sense of his own inadequacies. What lies 'behind' them is not the secret gem of an endangered self but the blind craving of the ego for gratification: 'The distinction between children and adults, while probably useful for some purposes, is at bottom a specious one, I feel. There are only individual egos, crazy for love' ('Me and Miss Mandible', *CBDC*, p. 108).

But, in spite of a fairly consistently passive attitude, the subject experiences a deep sense of alienation. His major discovery seems to be not so much that he is inadequate but that our culture and society are based on illusions and lies. In particular, he loses confidence in signs, having realized what we could call their arbitrary nature and their liability to being manipulated:

> I believed that because I had obtained a wife who was made up of wife-signs (beauty, charm, softness, perfume, cookery)

I had found love. Brenda, reading the same signs that have now misled Miss Mandible and Sue Ann Brownly, felt she had been promised that she would never be bored again. All of us, Miss Mandible, Sue Ann, myself, Brenda, Mr Goodykind, still believe that the American flag betokens a kind of general righteousness.

But I say, looking about me in this incubator of future citizens, that signs are signs, and that some of them are lies. This is the great discovery of my time here. ('Me and Miss Mandible', *CBDC*, p. 109)

*

This discovery may cause feelings of alienation and aloneness, of depression and yearning. But what is remarkable is that such feelings always remain, in Barthelme's fiction, somewhat unformed, in a nascent state, likely to evolve into something else, perhaps the very opposite emotional state. It is as if the 'destabilization' of signs had to be reappraised, to be seen not as the cause, but as an expression, of a more fundamental instability.

A good case in point is the Robert Kennedy figure, in the story 'Robert Kennedy Saved from Drowning', whose reactions are difficult to predict and catalogue because he himself is unsure about them, about his own role(s) and his exact emotional states. What emerges is an 'uncaused, vacant, a general anguish', a sense of variable, unpredictable moodiness. The story, from this point of view, is one of the most successful explorations of the epistemological uncertainty that affects Barthelme's world. Signs and feelings are either one way or the other; the subject oscillates between opposites:

He is neither abrupt with nor excessively kind to associates. Or he is both abrupt and kind.

The telephone is, for him, a whip, a lash, but also a conduit for soothing words, a sink into which he can hurl gallons of syrup if it comes to that.

He reads quickly, scratching brief comments ('Yes', 'No') in corners of the paper. He slouches in the leather chair, looking about him with a slightly irritated air for new visitors, new difficulties. He spends his time sending and receiving messengers.

'I spend my time sending and receiving messengers,' he

says. 'Some of these messages are important. Others are not.'
('Robert Kennedy Saved from Drowning', *UPUA*, p. 33)

At the end of the story, Barthelme has K. discuss the French writer Georges Poulet and his definition of the Marivaudian being – a discussion in which it seems possible to see an approximation of the 'Barthelmean being', of what we might call the subject of his fictions:

> The Marivaudian being is, according to Poulet, a pastless futureless man, born anew at every instant. The instants are points which organize themselves into a line, but what is important is the instant, not the line. The Marivaudian being has in a sense no history. Nothing follows from what has gone before. He is constantly surprised. He cannot predict his own reaction to events. He is constantly being *overtaken* by events. A condition of breathlessness and dazzlement surrounds him. In consequence he exists in a certain freshness which seems, if I may say so, very desirable. This freshness Poulet, quoting Marivaux, describes very well. (*UPUA*, p. 44)

There is no doubt that in this case a very strong element of fantasy is at work, and this element runs through many of the stories, attempting to hold together the irreconcilable, to shore up the fragments and contradictions: the alertness and the bewilderment, the lack of a sense of history but also the ability to see in the instant, 'which surges out of nothingness and which ends in dream, an intensity and depth of significance which ordinarily attaches only to the whole of existence' (*UPUA*, p. 43). It is, in one aspect, a kind of existential epistemology, an art of living and knowing as a high-wire act. But, at the same time, the exploration of the distance that separates sign from meaning, image from object, the emphasis on the contradictions and the discontinuity, are characteristic of an allegorical stance and, beyond that, of a post-modernist aesthetic.[11] We do not find here – as we do in Thomas Pynchon's work, for instance – the unifying element provided by a rampant paranoia, the sense that everywhere there are secret but powerfully articulated systems at work. Rather, what comes to the fore is a discourse that reiterates the unreadability, the obscurity, the *unheimlich* nature of opposed signals or meanings: a discourse that nevertheless persists in performing what is at the same time shown to be impossible. 'Robert Kennedy Saved from Drowning' is told by a first-person narrator who is, by his own admission, 'a notoriously poor observer'. What is problematized, then, is not simply the failure to decipher and narrate the subject or referent (the hypothetical 'Robert Kennedy'), but the activity of reference itself, the possibility of situating any referent of a discourse. This does not mean that the story becomes self-referential, self-sufficient; that would be in fact a typical modernist attitude. But the deconstructive impulse of post-modernist texts has little in common with the confident irony of modernism, which never stops believing in its own power, even when at its grimmest. The post-modernist text resolves nothing, and denies self-sufficiency and autonomy. It presents antithetical meanings or postures, presents and explores the range of the antithesis, of the distance itself (the distance between signifier and referent, description and image, subject and self), and leaves the reader (the reading), as Roland Barthes puts it, 'suspended'. Suspension is a favourite strategy of post-modernist forms of expression, and its playful nature, especially in the essentially comic fiction of Donald Barthelme, should not obscure the fact that at stake is a radical questioning of the symbolic process itself.

*

Barthelme has several names for this condition of epistemological uncertainty, this challenge to the symbolic: brain damage, sadness, *Angst*, lack of *Angst*, tears (tears abound in his stories – in 'At the Tolstoy Museum', 'Views of my Father Weeping', and many others). It is as if some stabilizing, regulative element had been lost, and as if in consequence significance and feelings were floating around, unanchored by the 'normal' symbolic process.

Freudian psychology tells us that access to the symbolic is gained through what it calls 'primal repression'. Roughly summarized, the process that determines the subject's access to language is a passage from a primitive stage in which the son occupies – or desires to occupy – the position of the real father and is therefore in unbearable competition with him, to a symbolic identification with the Father, the symbolic or dead father, or figure of the Law.[12] The outcome of this complex (and perhaps mythic) operation is to make possible the emergence of meaning and of further symbolic operations (such as articulate speech), to pass from a world of pure difference and meaningless oscillation to a world of ordered, 'anchored' signification. The so-called 'paternal metaphor', when it is successful (that is to say, when identification with the real father no longer obtains), acts as an anchor, a 'ballast', and allows the primitive material to be structured by the symbolic process of language. When it is *not* completely successful, as in the case of psychotic subjects, this process is affected, and it becomes impossible to distinguish between the symbol and the thing symbolized; what has not been successfully repressed or made symbolic returns or threatens to return under the form of hallucination.

This brief theoretical excursion confirms what the reader experiences when reading Barthelme: what is at stake behind the whimsy, the slapstick, the pop surrealism, concerns the symbolic itself – in particular, through the omnipresent figure of the father. But what Barthelme (who is quite well read in psychology) explores is not the thematic aspect of the figure as much as the area of symbolic uncertainty, of epistemological and psychic tensions between consciousness, hallucination and fantasy, between the symbolic order of intelligible discourse and the chaos of the non-symbolized.

In 'Views of My Father Weeping' one of the two alternating story lines is a quest for the truth about the father's death – a quest that is constantly foiled. The other consists in a series of visions, dreams or hallucinations of the father, who keeps returning and disturbing the son's emotional and symbolic order. The father, neither alive nor dead, is weeping silently as in a dream. He is the narrator's father, and not his father (he is 'Tom's father, Phil's father, Pat's father, etc.'. 'It is someone's father. That much is clear. He is fatherly'; *CL*, p. 7). His presence/absence triggers conflicting affects, denials and reminiscences, painful emotions which the narrator is unwilling or unable to turn away from him. But the question of the father here is not merely that of fascination with origins, another version of the old identity problem. Barthelme in fact presents a state halfway between mourning and melancholia, in which the ego loses its self-respect, in which 'one part of the ego sets itself over against the other, judges it critically, and, as it were, looks upon it as an object'.[13] Anxiety and depression result from the critical gaze of this part of the ego which sets itself up as a kind of censorious superego, an awesome and stern father. By the same token, the superego, no longer playing its tradi-

tional role as a protection, a reassurance against the fear of death and destruction, thus increases the panic. Barthelme's stories are often, from this point of view, attempts (sometimes funny, sometimes pathetic) to stage this situation and possibly exorcize it. We said that the result was halfway between grief and melancholia: as in grief, there is indeed an 'act of mourning' taking place, a withdrawing of the libido from the father-figure, an attempt to detach oneself by various means from the memory of the loss. But at the same time this affective energy does not seem to find new objects to attach itself to. It is 'withdrawn into the ego', where it floats freely, at times erupting in wild outbursts of emotions, at times hungrily, maniacally seeking something it can fasten on to.

This is not to say that Barthelme's texts ought to be reduced to this schema, but rather that their very diversity, their surface discrepancy, has a coherence – one or several unifying principles – which has often been denied by the commentators. In this respect, *The Dead Father* is a central text, the slow comic pageant of the Father, 'Dead, but still with us, still with us, but dead' (*DF*, p. 3), a guided tour of the inner workings of the *Ur*-father, organs and lusts, feelings and prohibitions, an indefinitely protracted burial. It is precisely an act of mourning that is presented, the metaphor made real with immense psychological acumen.[14] Witness, for instance, the 'Manual for sons' section, which explains exactly how the symbolic process works (and fails):

> Fatherless now, you must deal with the memory of a father. Often that memory is more potent than the living presence of a father, is an inner voice commanding, haranguing, yes-ing and no-ing – a binary code, yes no yes no yes no yes no, governing your every, your slightest movement, mental or physical. At what point do you become yourself? Never wholly, you are always partly him. (*DF*, p. 144)

Once a son, always a son ... a notion the Dead Father expresses in his own blunt way: 'A son can never, in the fullest sense, become a father. Some amount of amateur effort is possible. A son may after honest endeavour produce what some people might call, technically, children. But he remains a son. In the fullest sense' (*DF*, p. 33). Such is the organization that lies at the back of many stories, and accounts for the many oscillations, shifts of identity, the endless masquerading, masking and duplication. There is no hope, as Barthelme reminds us in another story, 'Daumier', that the self will ever be satisfied, because it was designed to be insatiable, 'always, always hankering' (*S*, p. 161). The self cannot be escaped, but it can, with ingenuity and hard work, be distracted. 'There are always openings, if you can find them, there is always something to do' (*S*, p. 18). One of the things that can be done is to construct imaginary selves, substitutes, surrogates, monsters, schizoid projections of ourselves, without the help of which we could not 'run the risk of acting, the risk of risk' ('Subpoena', *S*, p. 114).

4

BARTHELME'S
CODES OF TRANSACTION

Barthelme's fiction – rather like Beckett's – does point in the direction of a theoretical reconstruction of the self; this is a comic enterprise, however, and is undercut by one of Barthelme's favourite strategies of displacement and defence, his constant irony. His irony is, as we have seen, a generator of fiction, but when applied to the psychological and historical world it becomes part of the complicated game of the troubled subject. A good example of this is his story 'The Sandman', in *Sadness*, which consists of a letter written by a girl's boyfriend to her analyst. It is a funny letter, which displays Barthelme's thorough knowledge of psychoanalysis but also his ambivalent position towards it.

In 'The Sandman', the author of the letter writes to explain why he supports his friend's wish to terminate the analysis and buy a piano instead; he proceeds to expose the power game that underlies the process of psychoanalysis. He calls the analyst 'the Sandman' in reference, he says, to the old rhyme ('Sea-sand does the Sandman bring / Sleep to the end of Day / He dusts the children's eyes with sand / And steals their dreams away' (*S*, p. 86); but it is also a reference to Freud's use of the Sandman figure, which he borrowed from E. T. A. Hoffmann's famous tale 'The Sandman'.[15] The game of allusions and references is carried further when the author uses psychoanalytic literature against the analyst, quoting from articles in professional journals. The boyfriend is in effect challenging the methodology of the analyst – his rigid ego psychology and its underlying norms of behaviour, his desire to 'stabilize' Susan. This, if we bear in mind the author's own unhappy experience at the hands of a righteous 'liberal' analyst, can, of course, be construed as an indictment. The ironic refutation of the reductive practices of the analyst is forceful, and so is the act of love and total acceptance of the other which is put in its place. But the irony is both enhanced and undercut by the fact that in the process the narrator shows considerable analytic knowledge and skill (his observations would place him as a Freudian phenomenologist, not surprisingly for a writer who here and elsewhere quotes from Biswanger, Ehrenzweig, Ricœur and *Phenomenological Psychology*). His interpretations of voyeurism and creativity, in particular, are the standard ones. What comes out of the discussion of the case of Susan is a plea for the integrity of the self against stabilization, violent integration or escapism.

Beyond the anecdote and the little theoretical excursion, there remains a lesson for the artist. The lesson concerns not only creation itself (here, a characteristic way of writing stories) but also a way of being in the world (the characteristic 'Barthelmean' being):

> Let me point out, if it has escaped your notice, that what an artist does, is fail. Any reading of the literature (I mean the theory of artistic creation), however summary, will persuade you instantly that the paradigmatic artistic experience is that of failure. The actualization fails to meet, equal, the intuition. (*S*, p. 91)

What the individual is left with is the sense of his own energy, of his existential and intellectual creativity and integrity, with the inevitable ups and downs an uncompromising awareness brings about. But this seemingly self-centred consciousness leads to new developments in Barthelme's work, of a technical as well as of a psychological nature – as can be seen in more recent work, such as *Great Days* (1979).

*

Apart from its constant inventiveness in the use of language and fictional forms, Barthelme's writing has impressed its readers with the accuracy of the commentary on American life it provides. His work is, indeed, especially in collections such as *City Life* and *Sadness*, a *critique de la vie quotidienne* of urban civilization in the USA. This has been amply documented by critics and by the writer himself, but one particular aspect of it is worth pursuing here: the interactions, the interface in his work between the individual psychology and the social or political element. There is a formulation of this in 'The Sand-man':

> What do you do with a patient who finds the world unsatis-factory? The world *is* unsatisfactory; only a fool would deny it. . . . Susan's perception that America has somehow got hold of the greed ethic and that the greed ethic has turned America into a tidy little hell is not, I think, wrong. (*S*, p. 93)

This remark, probably because it is formulated by a character whose explicit theme is a critique of strategies of escapism and adjustment, has a liberal modernist ring to it. But, if Barthelme deserves to be called, as he often is, a post-modernist, it is because of the way he captures and presents obliquely aspects of what we might call the *cultural unconscious* of America. We say 'cultural unconscious' not only to avoid the very dubious word 'collective' but also because other concepts, like 'ideol-ogy' or 'epistemology', are perhaps too heavy, too formidable for what we have in mind. But it is clearly something of the same nature, the sort of analysis of the forces at work in society as well as in discourse which Jean-François Lyotard and Jean Baudrillard, among others, have been conducting over the last decade.[16]

Barthelme's fictions are crisscrossed by a bewildering cir-culation of flows and forces: money, speech, affects, informa-tion in the form of quotations, clichés and noise (the opposite of information) are caught in a process of continuous symbolic exchange. At times, especially in the early stories, discourse is explicitly translated into monetary terms (either because it is worth so much on the market, say in the media – as in 'A Shower of Gold', *CBDC*; or more generally because language and speech are a commodity, a currency that can be exchanged against almost anything, as in 'The Balloon', *UPUA*). Like money, discourse can suffer devaluation because of bad cur-rency: *dreck*, scraps, clichés, waste. Or else excessive accu-mulation and acceleration of exchanges can create an inflation-ary whirlwind, leading to giddiness and panic. Barthelme, in stories such as 'The Rise of Capitalism' (*S*) or 'Paraguay', is a remarkable analyst of the uncharted waters of post-industrial capitalism. What makes him so intuitively accurate, and so close to the more theoretical work of, say, Baudrillard, is that the economic or monetary metaphor or level is always bound up with the psychic element. Discourse, reduced to pure exchange value, stripped of all referentiality, may suddenly regain objectality or use value because of scarcity or unexpected difficulties in the utterence – as in the wonderful scene from 'A Picture History of the War' quoted earlier – which characterize our retentiveness, the anality and anxiety of our greed ethic. But it is never long before it loses its objecthood and becomes an empty sign system, in the blanks between words, in the aimless repetitions and fruitless rewordings, the disjunction and monotony that characterize the obsessional neurosis of the culture.

In this respect, Donald Barthelme has affinities with William Gaddis, especially with his novel *JR* (1975) – except, of course, that with Gaddis the shattering of codes is more complete, the text becomes purely transactional, and words are only so many particles in a network of flows, totally and instantaneously exchangeable with others: stocks, automobile traffic, TV images, static, scraps of music, and so on. The human voice, like currency, is the vehicle for an infinite exchangeability, void of all use value, in which exchanges create only additional exchange. The apparent differences in style between the two writers (the extreme length of Gaddis's novel, and its slow accretion over the years, as opposed to Barthelme's short fictions, and their appearance in periodicals, for example) should not conceal the deeper analogies. If there is a real difference, it lies in the fact that Gaddis carries the 'destabilization' of discourse, its decodification, much further. Barthelme – and this is perhaps one of his limitations – shifts his ground quite often, begins again from new positions, falls back on old dispositions. Precisely because his fictions are short, the strategies are more visible – indeed, they sometimes call attention to themselves. This is not necessarily a liability, since it is one of the constitutive aspects of Barthelme's post-modernism, giving his work a contemporary (one could almost say fashionable) self-reflexiveness and sense of the cultural *ambiance*. Besides, the brevity of the form generates intense situations, humour and the satisfaction (for reader and writer alike) of something having been, as Barthelme puts it, 'completed'.

But the feeling of strategies of manipulation is never very far away. Barthelme is ever the gamester, the master of language games which often carry over into self-parody and to the edge of self-destruction. One of the favourite games is in the form of dialogue. Dialogue here is seldom 'conversational' in the traditional sense; rather, it serves as a generator of fiction: a word, a statement, is offered, tossed about, picked up, played with, and yields a certain amount of free association, self-confession or pure verbal energy. This can be considered the more 'successful' form of 'conversation', when a certain smoothness of rhythm is achieved, a lubrication, a music, as is the case in the voice stories of *Great Days*. But such 'felicitous trularity' is not always so easily achieved. A complicity has to be established, a framework set up. That is why conversations often borrow ritualized forms: the confession, the question-and-answer test, the psychoanalytic session, the interview, and so on. All those situations have in common an informational or therapeutic objective, as well as a power relation more or less explicitly realized. But, most of all, they provide the space and the pretext for a discourse free of the requirements of 'normal' conversation, free to indulge in all its obsessions, repetitions, fantasies and self-defences:

> Q: Are you bored with the question-and-answer form?
> A: I am bored with it but I realize that it permits many valuable omissions: what kind of day it is, what I'm wearing, what I'm thinking. That's a very considerable advantage, I would say
> Q: I believe in it ('The Explanation', *CL*, p. 80)

Every conversation is a form of mutual aggression and/or of mutual analysis. Sometimes this produces the standard rebellion of the 'analysand' against the 'analyst':

> Q: You could interest yourself in these interesting machines. They're hard to understand. They're time-consuming
> A: I don't like you
> Q: I sensed it
> A: These imbecile questions . . .
> Q: Inadequately answered . . .
> A: . . . imbecile questions leading nowhere . . .
> Q: The personal abuse continues
> A: . . . that voice, confident and shrill . . .
> Q (aside): He has given away his gaiety, and now has nothing ('Kierkegaard Unfair to Schlegel', *CL*, p. 99)

In the several stories based on a similar pattern, the answerer is a sensitive, depressed person, who believes in the power and

46

confusion of love, against the technocratic order of textbooks of all kinds, against the inquisitorial discourse of psychology, religion or 'science'. 'The Explanation' is particularly significant in this respect, since it stages the resistance of the 'answerer' to the questioner's technological cant and his attempts to manipulate him. The strategy is that of affects against hyperrationality, of 'madness' against 'the reign of right reason' (the content of which, according to the A figure, is rhetoric):

Q: I have a number of error messages I'd like to introduce here and I'd like you to study them carefully . . . they're numbered. I'll go over them with you: undefined variable . . . improper use of hierarchy . . . missing operator . . . mixed mode, that one's particularly grave . . . argument of a function is fixed-point . . . improper character in constant . . . improper fixed-point constant . . . improper floating-point constant . . . invalid character transmitted in sub-program statement, that's a bitch . . . no END statement
A: I like them very much
Q: There are hundreds of others, hundreds and hundreds
A: You seem emotionless
Q: That's not true
A: To what do your emotions . . . adhere, if I can put it that way? ('The Explanation', *CL*, p. 79)

Confronted here are two modes of scanning the real and the discourses that attempt to structure it. And, in the comic enunciation of faulty transmission of information, the answerer probably sees, as the reader does, nothing but fantastic possible worlds of fiction, lusciously, parasitically proliferating. But, ultimately, his challenge is not even to the other as agent of organized technocratic power. Rather it is addressed to him, as the end of the quotation makes clear, as an agent and a victim of the tedium of repetition, of the slow death of non-feeling. 'The Catechist' (in *Sadness*) gives a particularly successful staging of this symbolic situation. A priest who has fallen in love with a woman is being questioned and instructed day after day by a catechist:

The catechist opens his book. He reads: *'The apathy of the*

listeners. The judicious catechist copes with the difficulty.'
He closes the book.

I think: Analysis terminable and interminable. I think: Then she will leave the park looking backward over her shoulder.

He says: 'And the guards, what were they doing?' I say: 'Abusing the mothers'

'You wrote a letter?'

'Another letter'

'Would you say, originally, that you had a vocation? Heard a call?'

'I heard many things. Screams. Suites for unaccompanied cello. I did not hear a call.'

'Nevertheless —'

'Nevertheless I went to the clerical-equipment store and purchased a summer cassock and a winter cassock. . . .' (*S*, p. 123)

*

The change that takes place with *Great Days* is that the dialogues seem to free themselves of the question-and-answer pattern and become more complex procedures. At the same time, the relations between the two voices are no longer ruled by aggression or investigation principles as in the examples above. Has conversation, then, become, as one of the speakers in *Great Days* puts it, a 'nonculminating kind of ultimately affectless activity'? (*GD*, p. 159). Yes, in the sense that play has been substituted for confrontation, analysis and anxiety. As the same speaker says to his partner, 'I respect your various phases. Your sweet, even discourse' (*GD*, p. 159). This is not to say that Barthelme's later stories have become gentle psalmodies of love. If love does figure prominently in them, it is in a somewhat ambiguous way, and always with the peculiar edge of his humour: 'Love, the highest form of human endeavour', but also 'Love which allows us to live together male and female in small grubby apartments that would only hold one sane person, normally' ('The Leap', *GD*, p. 152).

But that is only one of the reasons why the later stories cannot be termed 'affectless' in any way. Affects, as always, are pervasive. The difference with earlier fictions is that they have become so pervasive that they are now the very object of the language games being played. 'Morning' begins as an exorcism of fear ('Say you're frightened. Admit it –'). 'The Leap' is a ritual in preparation for the great day, the day 'we make the leap to faith'. 'Great Days', similarly, is a ritual review and exorcism of past behaviour leading to the final promise to love and remember:

— There's a thing the children say
— What do the children say?
— They say: Will you always love me?
— Always
— Will you always remember me?
— Always (*GD*, pp. 171–2)

But, beyond such apparent 'culminations', a lot of 'nonculminating' activity does go on in the *Great Days* texts. In fact, their structural principle is the performative mode. Microsequence after micro-sequence, games are played, promises made, inventions, rituals, exorcisms performed. Unidentified voices perform, act. In 'The New Music', the two voices 'doing mamma' fall into it like musicians going through a routine number. The texts become the record of the activity of voices; more accurately, they *are* the activities themselves.[17]

Barthelme's success in this new form of experimentation is brilliant: the stories are, one feels, 'purified' of the whimsy and of the sometimes facile post-modernist chic of the earlier collections. They are also purified in the sense that all trace of narrative 'dross' has been removed from them. The surprising fact is that this genuinely innovative technique also remains accessible and enjoyable to the reader. With the precision and insight of the master craftsman, Barthelme has refined and inflected his technique, emphasizing the more creative elements of his earlier work and discarding the rest, and working into it the dynamism of the performative mode. One is reminded of Samuel Beckett's wonderful rebound in *Company* (1980), of his cunning use, once more, of the voice, of what in recent theories has the highest creative potential, the verbal inventiveness, the sense of play and transaction. Such a keen sense of transactions and strategies (will Barthelme ever write a play, one wonders?) radically displaces the question of metafiction. The notion itself always had, it seems, something formalistic and limiting about it. Of course, it is true that one aspect of some of Barthelme's stories does concern itself with the art and the act of telling stories, of performing discursive acts of all kinds. And their modernity certainly has to do with the way the reader finds himself actively enlisted in them, his alertness and creativity being part and parcel of a successful performance of the text, of its being 'completed'. But then this can be said of almost every good writer, even though the modalities, of course, can be widely different. And metafiction, if it is to be successful as such, must carry the self-reflexiveness and the self-performance much further – as, for example, Italo Calvino has done in his recent meta-novel to end all meta-novels, *Se per una notte d'inverno, un viaggiatore* (*If On A Winter's Night A Traveller*, 1981). Clearly, Barthelme's originality and effectiveness do not rest on such brittle notions. His is a genuinely inventive and innovative fiction, for the many reasons we have suggested (and, no doubt, for several others as well).

5

BARTHELME IN THE ART GALLERY

Barthelme's work, as we observed in Chapter 1, proceeds by a 'disenchantment of symbols' towards a parodic process of interpretative exhaustion, which then seems surprisingly inexhaustible. His process of linguistic saturation, which apparently precludes all possible communication between author and reader, in fact kindles the imagination and makes it capable of evolving or registering unprecedented images. While more rhetorical discourses address our reason and curb our imagination, Barthelme's do not – the figures of speech do not boost the signified and lull the imagination to sleep, but instead generate increased imaginative activity. For example, when we read about a girl's 'lustrous sexuality' ('A Film', *S*, p. 77) or of a 'herd of *au pair* girls' which must be taken 'to the railhead intact in both mind and body' ('Daumier', *S*, p. 164), or again about 'a river of girls and women' (*SW*, p. 15), we may not be clear what meanings are being promoted by the metaphors; but what matters is that vivid images, which our minds find hard to apprehend, are magically created. These images, triggered by the words 'lustrous', 'herd' and 'river', overshadow the objects they are apparently meant to characterize. With Barthelme, images are never purely ornamental or pedagogical. They are not meant to prod the slumbering reader but to produce a kind of seismic shock: the gap between comparer and compared appears so vast that we are momentarily perplexed and find it difficult to achieve a degree of equanimity (as Barthelme would phrase it). In our attempt to bridge this gap, we may resort to all kinds of foolish devices – like the Dead Father, who, finding himself 'on the wrong side of the Styx', uses an ingenious if painful stratagem to cross to the other side:

> Uncoiling my penis, then in the dejected state, I made a long cast across the river, sixty-five meters I would say, where it snagged most conveniently in the cleft of a rock on the farther shore. Thereupon I hauled myself hand-over-hand 'midst excruciating pain as you can imagine through the raging torrent to the other bank. (*DF*, p. 38)

In a somewhat similar fashion, the reader who does not wish to remain in a quandary has constantly to make great efforts of the imagination in the course of reading Barthelme's fictions; the ability to create or reflect new images is required the whole time.

The process whereby such fictions manage to trigger vivid images is not easy to understand. For instance, in the case of the au-pair girls driven around the country, we are reminded both of the celebrated cattle drives of the 1860s and of the shipping of wicked women from Europe to the east coast and then on to the west. We are also led to contemplate the idea that the modern practice of inviting foreign girls to stay with the family and work for their upkeep can be likened to the older practice and often involves a sexual commerce of some kind. The French phrase which has been retained to label this practice is, in itself, somewhat disquieting; the fact that, at first, many of the au-pair girls in Britain or the United States were from France is not a sufficient justification. Is it perhaps a sign that this modern trade is unconsciously felt to be equivocal? After all, the French have always had the reputation of being a licentious people. In this case, however, it is the British or the Americans who are licentious: they are the ones who exploit foreign girls under cover of teaching them the language; they are also the ones who retain the French expression. We suddenly realize that this expression could be read differently, as '*au père*' (same pronunciation). Au-pair girls temporarily belong *au père*: they are exotic mistresses acquired free of charge.

Barthelme may not have had all these things in mind when he wrote this passage, and he may have thought of many other things which this interpretation has failed to elucidate. It does not matter; this was simply an attempt to show how readers desperately rack their brains and strain their imagination to exorcize the spell cast by a disturbing metaphor or comparison. This example proves, moreover, that Barthelme's figures of speech are not being used rhetorically: this passage is about neither cattle drives nor au-pair girls, but about both at the same time. One cannot decide which is the comparer, which the compared. That is precisely how a painter or caricaturist like Daumier (who is supposed to be the subject of this fiction) usually works: his paintings are not meaningful only in relation to the reality they represent or parody; they have a value and a relevance of their own, for otherwise they would cease to be valuable or meaningful when the reality they claim to represent has disappeared.

Judging from this example, it would be tempting to say that the vividness of an image, in these fictions, is due to the ambiguity of the words themselves and to the unusual pairing of words. However, as many fictions in the later collections (*Amateurs*, especially) testify, not all word-games generate such striking images. As the 'Daumier' anecdote seems to suggest, it is not so much the word-game as the hidden subject, sex, which accounts for the vividness of the image. In the same fiction there is another passage where this subject is more explicitly mentioned: 'the shoulders on her were as tempting as sex crimes' (*S*, p. 169). The sexual reference is a great deal less patent, though, in the following passage:

> Outside his window five-year-old Priscilla Hess, square and squat as a mailbox (red sweater, blue lumpy corduroy pants), looked around poignantly for someone to wipe her overflowing nose. There was a butterfly locked inside that mailbox, surely; would it ever escape? Or was the quality of mailboxness stuck to her forever, like her parents, like her name? ('The Piano Player', *CBDC*, p. 19)

The comparison seems to have been suggested at first by the girl's shape, but then we find out that it is probably the colour of her clothes that triggered it off. The comparison was not, therefore, as extravagant (arbitrary) as it seemed, but was more or less dictated by 'reality' itself (or perhaps the little girl deliberately dressed to look like a mailbox). Towards the end of the passage, this comparison expands yet further: the little girl is like a mailbox not only from the outside but also from the inside. We wonder, suddenly, if her 'mailboxness' is perhaps simply due to her sex: as a girl, she can be thought of as a 'malebox'. This is a great deal more than a gratuitous word-game; the vividness of the image depends as much on the disquieting referent (sex), which our unconscious probably senses immediately in the word 'mailbox', as on the rhetorical feat (the distance between 'little girl' and 'mailbox').

The latter example also suggests that the quality of the image is created not only by the specific nature of the referent – be it sex, or whatever – but also by the wavering of our mind and imagination between two interpretations, the linguistic and the existential. This is even more obvious in the following passage: 'In the larger stores silence (damping materials) is sold in paper sacks like cement. . . . The extension of white noise to the home by means of leased wire from a central generating point has been useful, Herko says' ('Paraguay', *CL*, p. 27). Linguistically speaking, two word pairs sound unacceptable: 'silence . . . is sold', and 'white noise'. The reality they presuppose seems quite alien to our own: in our world, only quantifiable objects or goods can be sold, and only noises and images can be transmitted on a cable, not silence, because it is not quantifiable and therefore economically worthless. These verbal-cum-scientific tricks combine to create a very strong image, 'white noise', which is without referent and has nothing to do with its opposite, 'noise' – another word for 'nuisance', as information theory reminds us. Barthelme's statement sounds like a parody of the proverb 'speech is silver, silence is gold', except that the colours do not perfectly match.

*

It should be clear by now why Barthelme's technique has been labelled as non-rhetorical, post-Saussurian or post-Freudian. Until the middle of the twentieth century, Western writers generally considered language as an instrument, a vehicle by which to convey their original ideas and stored-up images. Naturally, writing practice did not always conform to the avowed theory, and writers frequently gave free rein to their unconscious in word-games. Now this theory has been emphatically rejected; we know that language cannot be used as a mere instrument because, on the one hand, it has a logic of its own and, on the other, our unconscious constantly punctures it.

It may be useful at this point to remember the fate of *The Pilgrim's Progress*. Originally this book was intended to be essentially didactic. However, after it was published the religious establishment objected to it on the grounds that the story tended to capture the reader's imagination too much and therefore did not properly serve its intended, more elevated purpose. Closer to us, we find the strange case of *Lolita*. Everybody agreed that the novel was beautifully written and contained unforgettable images. But the moral establishment (including many 'learned readers') objected to it because it was anti-didactic and obscene. As John Ray, the naïve editor, puts it in his foreword, Humbert 'is abnormal. He is not a gentleman. But how magically his singing violin can conjure up a tendresse, a compassion for Lolita that makes us entranced with the book while abhorring its author!'[18] For John Ray and most readers, it is utterly shocking that good writing is not being used to serve a good cause. Barthelme's fictions have not elicited the same reactions, because they can be read as iconoclastic and therefore didactic to a certain extent, but they are essentially based on the same principles as these two celebrated books. They free the reader's intelligence and imagination from the dictatorship of the established representations of reality, from the ascendancy of hallowed values, and somehow ('the great "somehow" of dreams', as Nabokov phrases it[19]) get through to his unconscious, where the most vivid images can be triggered off and stored away. This shameless outpouring of crazy ideas, outrageous word-plays and surrealistic images weakens the reader's defences and invites him to let himself go.

For all we know, these fictions may act as a marvellous antidote to repression: they temporarily deliver us from our inhibitions and take us to another planet on which language is only a sumptuous toy. Gradually Barthelme makes us capable of accepting on trust such extravagant images as a city of churches or 'a pornographic pastry' (*SW*, p. 35). The problem of truthfulness, which, according to Todorov, plays such an important part in gothic fiction, does not arise here for a moment. Here, for example, is the opening of 'The Glass Mountain':

1. I was trying to climb the glass mountain.
2. The glass mountain stands at the corner of Thirteenth Street and Eighth Avenue.
3. I had attained the lower slope.
4. People were looking up at me.
5. I was new in the neighborhood. (*CL*, p. 59)

We do not marvel at the sight of the Glass Mountain in the centre of Manhattan, any more than we would at the sight of a skyscraper. The 'reality' of this wonder is taken for granted – as was the transformation of a man into a beetle in Kafka's *Metamorphosis*. This is exactly how things happen in our dreams: it is enough that we imagine this or that weird object for it to exist momentarily. When the dream is over, the object *qua* object disintegrates, as did the most trivial things on Borges' idealistic planet of Tlön when people stopped thinking about them, but the object *qua* image endures. It seems that the vividness of such dream images is in direct proportion to their ephemeralness and precariousness, like those rare flowers which blossom only a few hours every ten years.

This 'suspension of disbelief', which makes it possible for such extraordinary images to bloom, seems to be facilitated by certain stratagems and artifices, like the violation of scientific or technical principles – as in the following examples:

> Today we filmed fear, a distressing emotion aroused by impending danger, real or imagined. ('A Film', *S*, p. 75)

> This aircraft is powered by twelve rubber bands, each rubber band thicker than a man's leg . . . ('A Film', *S*, p. 82)

> – Went to the grocery store and Xeroxed a box of English muffins, two pounds of ground veal and an apple. In flagrant violation of the Copyright act. ('The New Music', *GD*, p. 21)

Technology (filming, flying, xeroxing) implies human intervention at many levels. It is based on a number of scientific laws which, because they were discovered after centuries of arduous research, seem unchangeable. Our imagination is fired by these technical marvels because we seem to have landed on another planet, and also because we have the impression that we could, in our turn, invent other planets simply by perverting this or that scientific law.

This pedagogical technique, which plays a very important part in science fiction, probably accounts also, to a certain extent, for the extraordinary success of surrealism. Until the surrealist movement, it was usually assumed that artistic creation was the privilege of exalted visionaries and that, no matter how hard one worked at it, one could never hope to create such beautiful objects or images unless one possessed a certain gift. Since surrealism, one has the impression that a system is available whereby any ordinary person can create strong and unprecedented images: all one has to do, apparently, is to use a collage technique of some sort to bring together objects that had never been seen side by side before. You don't have to be a genius to do that; all that appears to be required is that you be a handy technician. Naturally we are fooling ourselves if we believe that; but there is little doubt that fantasy plays an important part in the way we react to these fictions. Look, Barthelme seems to say, I am sure you could dream up such strange pairings as:

He began to trundle [the piano] across the room, and, after a slight hesitation, it struck him dead. ('The Piano Player', *CBDC*, p. 22)

The hospital refused to give him a disease. ('The Dragoon', *GP*, p. 78)

The bull begins to ring, like a telephone. ('The Wound', *A*, p. 17)

Kellerman knocks back the Beaujolais, tucks his naked father under his arm, and runs out the door. ('A Picture History of the War', *UPUA*, p. 128)

A number of nightingales with traffic lights tied to their legs flew past me. ('The Glass Mountain', *CL*, p. 63)

All these sentences make use of the collage technique and remind us at times of the testing of paradigms in linguistic textbooks: hospitals exist to provide a number of things but not diseases; a bull can low but it cannot ring; you can tuck a child under your arm but not your naked father, especially if he is a general in Napoleon's army.

The collage technique does not always produce the same effect, of course. What fascinates us in Barthelme's surrealistic images is the fact that they contain a strong oneiric element. Surrealism has often been said to be a highly intellectual form of art. What is probably meant is that, while surrealist art is not obviously more intellectual than realistic art, the audience must exert their minds a great deal more if they want to formulate an acceptable interpretation. Surrealistic fictions are crammed with phenomena which (it seems) can only be, in Freudian parlance, the product of primary processes; they do not seem to spring from an individual's conscious mind but from his unconscious – which makes them very disturbing, of

57

course. The 'learned reader' (who is usually a very sensible person) cannot accept what he fails to understand or master; like the analysand who is telling a dream to his analyst, the reader submits the images to a 'secondary processing' and blots out the elements that ruffled his imagination by rationalizing them. Traditionally, it had always been considered that such images could only be dreamt, not made up. It seems that Barthelme has mastered this difficult art, that he can extract anything he likes from his Mad Hatter's top hat. Very few people can attain such 'states of nonordinary reality', and we agree with him that, 'if just anybody did, by accident, blunder into a state of nonordinary reality, the anybody might bloody well regret it' ('The Teaching of Don B.', *GP*, p. 54). We feel that it may be too dangerous to give free rein to one's unconscious like this, and that madness may not be too far away.

*

Nowhere do we experience this feeling so intensely as in the 'illustrated' fictions. In many of these fictions, we find side by side a highly fragmented text and a seemingly random sequence of extravagant pictures which usually have nothing to do (apparently) with the text. We might return to 'Brain Damage'; here, in a fiction that precisely deals with, or rather simulates, madness, most of the pictures inserted between the fragments represent visions of panic. The classical statue (*CL*, p. 139), apparently a collage of two pictures, contrasts an image of intense drama with one of complete indifference (the boy who looks the other way at the left-hand corner). The weeping lady, in the next picture, seems to be related to the caption in block letters which immediately follows: 'WRITHING HOWLING MOANS WHAT RECOURSE?' (*CL*, p. 141); she is not a character in the story, however, but only a pictorial correlative. The children playing blindman's buff have no equivalent either in the story, but this image seems to be telling us something about the nature of madness. The last picture does not convey the same impression of panic, but it is even more disquieting: it represents a nun with an open umbrella who is partly concealed by the huge breast of a monumental woman. Though a nun is actually mentioned in the story, there is no echo to this scene anywhere. But then, Barthelme seems to suggest, madness ('brain damage') consists essentially in this inability to find coherence in the world: it cannot be described or analysed properly; it can only be mimicked or mirrored.

It would be wrong, however, totally to naturalize this fiction in psychiatric terms. As we have already said, Barthelme deliberately tries to do away with rhetoric and challenges us to produce our own interpretations, our own images. Remember Borges' story of Pierre Menard, the rewriter of *Don Quixote*. Barthelme's fictions are more like art galleries than lecture halls. It would be difficult, for instance, to read 'At the Tolstoy Museum' as a lecture on Tolstoy. At first the pictures ('Tolstoy's coat', 'Tolstoy as a youth', 'At Starogladkovskaya, about 1852', *CL*, pp. 43, 44, 46) seem to illustrate the text, but in fact they don't: Tolstoy's coat is three times as high as the Lilliputian visitors; Tolstoy as a youth looks strangely like a baby-faced Napoleon, with his unruly lock of hair; and we wonder if the bicycle represented in the third picture existed in Russia as early as 1852. Obviously this museum could not be a Tolstoy museum; it is more like an art gallery, each page being as it were a surrealistic composition. This is confirmed by the following drawings: 'The Anna-Vronsky Pavilion', in which actors seem to be performing a scene from *Anna Karenina* with an Italian décor; 'At the disaster (arrow indicates Tolstoy)', which pictures a ruinous palace with a number of tiny figures quite impossible to identify; and, finally, 'Museum plaza with monumental head (Closed Mondays)' (*CL*, pp. 48, 49, 50). The latter caption is as ambiguous as the picture itself, though in a different way: the word 'monumental' can mean either that the head is gigantic or that this is truly a monument (which cannot be, since Tolstoy's head appears only as a negative in the background); the parenthesis can refer to 'Museum', 'plaza' or 'monumental head'. The rational interpretation of the text becomes as problematical as that of the pictures; it is bound to reflect the desires of the interpreter as much as the intentions of the artist.

Barthelme's fictions, like Paul Delvaux's paintings, are maddening eye-traps: they cannot stand to be read or looked at, but seem to stare at us. In a Dali optical illusion like *Slave Market with the Invisible Bust of Voltaire*, we don't feel as if Voltaire were watching us from out of space, whereas in Delvaux's works, where the technique is apparently less elaborate, the naked women seem to be trying to outstare us with their wide gazing eyes and arrogant breasts. Likewise, Barthelme's fictions make us feel extremely uncomfortable. The perspective studies (present in 'At the Tolstoy Museum'), apparently lifted from a treatise by Brunelleschi or Ucello, which Barthelme has a fancy for (like Delvaux), produce a similar effect: we cannot enjoy them passively but are forced to position our eyes properly. We are caught in the pencilled web and seem unable to disentangle ourselves. In the second picture of 'The Flight of Pigeons from the Palace' – whose caption reads 'I put my father in the show, with his cold eyes. His segment was called, My Father Concerned About His Liver' (S, p. 128) – the huge liver perching on the pedestal, in the middle of the hall, is somewhat like a multifaceted eye or mirror reflecting the looks of the father, the arcades, the artist and, eventually, the reader too. Escher's lithograph entitled *Print Gallery* offers an even more eye-catching challenge: a young man is looking at a painting, in an art gallery, but the painting (in which a lady is staring at him from her window) nightmarishly expands to encompass the gallery and the young man himself.[20] The visitor is unwittingly caught in the painting he is admiring and cannot escape.

Barthelme, like Escher, paralyses our intelligence and lures us into entering his surrealistic world which has indeed very little to do with our own. He cleverly constructs 'surrogates', compelling images, through a series of displacements. The technique is extremely well depicted in 'Engineer-Private Paul Klee Misplaces an Aircraft between Milbertshofen and Cambrai, March 1916'. The painter has been asked to deliver three aircrafts to the front; as he walks out of a station restaurant, he discovers that an aircraft is missing. He is very annoyed, of course, but the 'puddle of canvas and loose rope' (S, p. 67) which has taken the place of the missing plane on the railroad car catches his artist's eye, and he starts sketching it. This gives him the idea of 'diddling the manifest'; after all, as the policemen who have been watching him recognize, 'his painter's skill . . . resembles not a little that of the forger' (S, p. 69). Changing a figure or a word on a manifest suddenly changes reality. As a result of all this, Klee will create a new work which will outlive the war: 'The war is temporary. But drawings and chocolate go on forever' (S, p. 70). As we read this text, we strain our inner eye to try to picture the drawing; we completely forget meanwhile that this is Barthelme's own invention. The more elusive the image is, the more difficult it is for the reader to find his way out of it and for the commentator to wind up his rambling analysis.

6

BARTHELME AND THE ESCHERIAN PERCEPTION

The extravagant manipulation of narrative strategies, the construction of vivid semantic images and the tactics of displacement do not necessarily preclude the unfolding of more or less linear stories – as the novels of Vladimir Nabokov, John Barth and even Thomas Pynchon testify. But they do make it difficult to study them narratologically. The famous narrative theories of Vladimir Propp and A. Greimas were founded on oral literature, or else on fairly primitive forms of written literature, like the folk-tale.[21] The texts they dealt with bore few traces of individual enunciation; this made it much easier to discriminate the story *per se*. But what has been found is that such theories are of little use with modernist and postmodernist texts, because they cannot take the mode of enunciation into proper consideration.

With many of Barthelme's fictions, the problem seems hardly worth raising, because there is no identifiable story, or, if there is, it is so circuitous that it flouts all the norms of the well-structured narrative. No matter how clever and useful, elsewhere, a theory like Greimas's may be, the fundamental concepts ('subject', 'object', 'donator', and so on) are not universals but reflect a given structure of reality based on metaphysical presuppositions (God is the ultimate donator, for example) and universalize an implied consensus. But it is precisely such a consensus that Barthelme cannot consent to – as he says in *Snow White*, 'It is unbearable, this consensus, this damned felicity' (*SW*, p. 66). Everything in life, and in books, is too predictable – as it has been for other contemporary authors – because we have heard or read too many stories. As Propp unwittingly proved, given a certain version of reality, the

61

number of stories that can be invented is limited. Even when a story is based on actual facts, it fails to sound really new because we cannot help tacking traditional narrative structures on to the new events. Barthelme is highly aware of these limitations; in *The Dead Father* Thomas says: 'No tale ever happened in the way we tell it . . . but the moral is always correct' (*DF*, p. 46). We take this to mean that the deciphering of events is always subject to our capacity to understand their relevance or their significance. Gombrich said practically the same thing, in *Art and Illusion*, about our way of deciphering drawings and paintings.

This conservative treatment of new facts is extremely well illustrated by 'The Balloon'. This disturbing story, which will be analysed more thoroughly later in this chapter, is about a huge balloon which appeared one day in the clear sky of Manhattan. Faced with this unaccounted-for object, the New Yorkers begin by trying out their learned discourses (journalistic, sociological, psychological, economic) in their attempt to naturalize it. For instance, we read: 'There was a certain amount of initial argumentation about the "meaning" of the balloon' (*UPUA*, p. 16) and 'The apparent purposelessness of the balloon was vexing' (*UPUA*, p. 17). Barthelme parodies the pompous discourses that contaminate the various layers of society; he even provides a few samples of bad literary reviews: 'monstrous pourings' (*UPUA*, p. 19); 'Has unity been sacrificed for a sprawling quality?' (*UPUA*, p. 20). This is nothing but an inventory of clichés. What Barthelme is suggesting is that the reactions of the New Yorkers are highly predictable: nothing is accepted on trust or taken for granted; every new phenomenon must be submitted to the test of science and reason. The event that baffles the mind and imagination must be brought down to acceptable dimensions by means of exhaustive argument.

Barthelme constantly denounces what he calls this ' "blanketing" effect of ordinary language' (*SW*, p. 96). We speak and write simply to coat things with meaning – to 'cosmeticize reality', as another character puts it ('Perpetua', *S*, p. 38). We do not use our creative power to develop other worlds in which our imagination could revel and be free, but simply try to fill the gaps in our representation of reality in order to make it less awesome. There is a crude way of reacting to this – iconoclastic aggression – but Barthelme rejects it: 'ANATHEMATIZATION OF

(*SW*, p. 178); it gives only the illusion of power and freedom, but, indirectly, it bolsters and boosts the consensus. What he feels is needed, as we have explained, is some kind of refined irony that is capable of 'depriving the object of its reality in order that the subject may feel free' ('Kierkegaard Unfair to Schlegel', *CL*, p. 88). Instead of naturalizing the puzzling object or phenomenon, Barthelme strives hard to make it even more baffling or esoteric. In his recent interview with Larry McCaffery, he explains that his fictions develop through a process of accretion:

> Barnacles growing on a wreck or a rock. If you have a wreck to begin with, that's a wonderful thing. I'd personally rather have a wreck than a ship that sails. Things attach themselves to wrecks. Strange fish find your wreck or rock to be a good feeding ground and after a while you've got a pretty interesting situation out of this wreck.[22]

You are not free to do what you like with 'a ship that sails' because it has an assigned place and function in the economic system, but you can do whatever comes to your mind with the worthless wreck. Barthelme's irony is not bitter or didactic; it is akin to Nabokov's gamesome parody.[23]

This supreme form of irony is the basis for this 'art of the possible, plus two' ('The Abduction from the Seraglio', *GD*, p. 93), which is somewhat like that of Daumier:

> It is easy to be satisfied if you get out of things what inheres in them, but you must look closely, take nothing for granted, let nothing become routine. You must fight against the cocoon of habituation which covers everything, if you let it. There are always openings, if you can find them. ('Daumier', *S*, p. 177)

Such is the technique used to invent surrogates, to create new objects with virtually nothing. The Dead Father was capable of fathering, upon a pretty girl called Tulla, 'the poker chip, the cash register, the juice extractor, the kazoo, the rubber pretzel, the cuckoo clock, the key chain, the dime bank, the pantograph, the bubble pipe' (*DF*, p. 36). At the sentence and paragraph level, this technique produces the extravagant images analysed earlier; at the textual level, it gives fragmented fictions. For the storyteller, 'the cocoon of habituation' is made of a number of narrative conventions of which we are now highly aware, thanks to the work of people like Propp. Barthelme strenuously fights against these conventions by constantly breaking the narrative line ('Brain Damage', 'Daumier', 'The Falling Dog'). The fragments can individually retain a semblance of unity ('The Phantom of the Opera's Friend', 'City Life'), but in many cases they don't. The reader feels extremely embarrassed; he has no idea what these fictions are about because there are just too many subjects evoked. For instance, is 'The Viennese Opera Ball' about childbirth, the Viennese Opera, the ball or literature? Is 'I Bought a City' (a fairly chronological fiction) a parody of city planning, or of leadership in general, or else a story of unrequited love? In Clarence Major's *Reflex and Bone Structure* there is a character who similarly will not focus.[24] There is no satisfactory way of summarizing such stories, since a narrative line always depends on the 'moral', a prime meaning – which is absent here.

Another device, which he uses particularly in *Great Days* ('The Crisis', 'The Apology', 'The New Music') and in *The Dead Father*, consists in writing a whole text in the form of a dialogue. What makes this technique particularly effective is the total absence of 'stage directions', so that it is practically impossible to identify the deictic co-ordinates: who are the characters, where are they, and when did the dialogue take place? Without such indications, any piece of recorded dialogue would be difficult to understand, but when transcribed it does not make any sense at all: we do not even know how many characters there are. This technique is the more compelling as it seems natural.[25] What the reader misses most, perhaps, in these fictions is not the deictic co-ordinates (who, when, where), but the illocutionary value of what is being said (the intended speech act behind the words: statement, complaint, promise, question, and so on). What do the characters actually have in mind? What do they want to achieve? In 'The Apology', for instance, where the situation is easy to picture (husband and wife arguing), one cannot easily understand the precise purpose of such statements as:

> – *William I'm sorry you don't ski and I'm sorry about your back and I'm sorry I invented bop jogging which you couldn't do! I'm sorry I loved Antigua! I'm sorry my mind*

wandered when you talked about the army! I am sorry I was
superior in argument! (*GD*, p. 17)

This goes on for two pages, while William keeps congratulating her on her performance, or talks about something else. One does not usually apologize for things one is not responsible for, for achieving positive things ('I'm sorry I invented bop jogging which you couldn't do'), or for just being better than somebody else. The text says a great deal more (and also less) than the sum of its words. Its ultimate meaning is partly undecidable because one cannot really imagine a situation in which it would apply.

The same effect is produced in 'Concerning the Bodyguard' by the long list of incongruous questions actually constituting the fiction, which begins like this: 'Does the bodyguard scream at the woman who irons his shirts? Who has inflicted a brown burn on his yellow shirt purchased expensively from Yves St Laurent? A great brown burn just over the heart?' (*GD*, p. 107). Many of the questions sound preposterous or of no interest whatsoever. One does not even know who is asking them and to whom, or for what purpose. The last two questions of this fiction read as a perfect non sequitur: 'Is it the case that, on a certain morning, the garbage cans of the city, the garbage cans of the entire country, are overflowing with empty champagne bottles? Which bodyguard is at fault?' (*GD*, p. 112). What could be the value and significance of questions that presuppose the existence of an impossible situation? Barthelme gives a new twist to his fiction and confers upon it a kind of iconic compactness which makes us unable to read it as a story. One finds a similar twist at the end of 'The Glass Mountain' with the sentence 'Nor are eagles plausible, not at all, not for a moment' (*CL*, p. 65). The narrator has claimed earlier that he had been taken to the top of the mountain by an eagle; now he suddenly erases this unlikely vehicle but still remains at the top of the glass mountain.

The anticlimactic endings make it difficult to summarize these fictions properly. With a linear narrative, the reader has the impression of understanding what the fiction is all about: there is a beginning, there is an end, and there is a moral. This traditional form of narrative is based on the same principles as daily communication: a piece of information is being conveyed by a discourse. In Barthelme's fictions, however, the principles that usually make for efficient communication are unceremoniously violated: there is no beginning, no end and, naturally, no moral. As in poetry, the words cease to be vehicular: they are like the numberless stones, with their various forms and colours, which are used in the construction of a building, or again the lines and pigments that enter into the composition of a painting. They are no longer limited or cramped by the code which traditionally programmed their meaning and value. It seems as if Barthelme has fulfilled his dream: 'I wanted to be a painter. They get away with murder in my view' ('See the Moon?', *UPUA*, p. 152). What he envies is this ability to create a work of art by simply picking up a worthless object, like a 'Baby Ruth wrapper', and foregrounding it merely by framing it. Question: who is the artist in this case, the innovative painter who framed the wrapper, or the hack artist who drew it? Neither, or both, or Barthelme who invented this work in the Andy Warhol style. Ideally, Barthelme suggests, we should not even raise this question; at the end of 'Daumier' he says: 'The self cannot be escaped, but it can be, with ingenuity and hard work, distracted' (*S*, p. 181). The self can fairly easily be distracted in paintings, but not so easily in literary works, where the strictly codified words always adhere very strongly to the individual who strung them out. Only by breaking the yarn, the narrative line, can this feat be achieved.

*

With this explanation, it becomes easier to understand why Barthelme has written mostly short fictions rather than long ones. In a novel, be its language as confusing as that of *Finnegans Wake*, or its sequences as contradictory as in Robbe-Grillet's *Jealousy*, one cannot help hearing a distinctive voice. On two occasions, however, Barthelme tried to challenge this supposed inevitability, and the results were the novels *Snow White* and *The Dead Father*. The theme of the former (the relationship between man and woman) is one of the most insistent of all in Barthelme's works. For example, 'Perpetua' and 'Critique de la Vie Quotidienne', in *Sadness*, or 'For I'm the Boy Whose Only Joy Is Loving You' and 'Will You Tell Me?', in *Come Back, Doctor Caligari*, are mostly unhappy love stories; 'The Piano Player', also in *Come Back, Doctor Caligari*, '110 West Sixty-First Street' and 'The Agreement', in *Amateurs*, deal with the problems children create between mother and father. On the surface, *Snow White*, like Clarence

Major's *Reflex and Bone Structure*, is a poignant statement about the heart-rending beauty of precarious love, and more precisely about the sublime remoteness and inaccessibility of the American woman. The most striking symbol of this inaccessibility is Snow White's hair, 'black as ebony', which two old men (who are reminiscent of the two lustful elders in the Susanna story in the Bible) observe 'tumbling from the window' (*SW*, p. 89). 'I hate to go away', says one of them, 'and leave all that hair hanging there unmolested as it were . . . but we have a duty to our families, and to the country's merchant fleet' (*SW*, p. 89). The seven dwarfs, though less decrepit, also desperately long to possess this hair and the girl, but they know all along that their dream will never come true because Snow White is always expecting her prince and cannot be satisfied with the paltry love they have to offer. Christopher Lasch brands this as a modern form of Bovaryism in the following terms:

> A latter-day Madame Bovary, Snow White is a typical victim of mass culture, the culture of commodities and consumerism with its suggestive message that experiences formerly reserved for those of high birth, deep understanding, or much practical acquaintance of life can be enjoyed by all without effort, on purchase of the appropriate commodity.[26]

This sociological reading of *Snow White* is somewhat reminiscent of John Ray's didactic reading of Humbert's story in *Lolita*. The text is erroneously taken as the discourse of the author; naturally, if this were the case, Barthelme would have failed to 'escape the self'.

There is, of course, another way of looking at Snow White – as the invention of a frustrated male, like Andromeda in John Barth's *Chimera* – but the idea apparently does not occur to Christopher Lasch, who insists that the American woman is to blame for the failures of American society (of the American male). This theory fails to take into account the formal aspects of this novel – the fact, for example, that the narrator seems to be one of the dwarfs. Snow White is not portrayed by an impartial narrator but by someone who is deeply involved with her. The situation, incidentally, is exactly the same in Major's *Reflex and Bone Structure*; the narrator feels he must have Cora – a modern Kore who keeps appearing and disappearing in the course of the novel – only for himself, and eventually kills her along with her lover. What Major and Barthelme are suggesting is that these mythical women are pure inventions not only of insecure males but also of highly imaginative artists who have fashioned them with the dregs of their (and society's) unfulfilled dreams. That does not make these women necessarily evil; on the contrary, they are dream creatures to whom a monument ought to be erected, modern love goddesses who deserve to be worshipped. At the end of Barthelme's novel, the leader of the dwarfs, Bill, he who could not stand to be touched, is hanged: 'He was guilty of vatricide and failure' (*SW*, p. 180). Snow White is not to blame for his shortcomings; as Barthelme phrased it two pages earlier: 'ANATHEMATIZATION OF THE WORLD IS NOT AN ADEQUATE RESPONSE TO THE WORLD' (*SW*, p. 178).

This conclusion, if it can be so called, reads very much like that of 'The Glass Mountain' or 'Concerning the Bodyguard'. It forces the wary reader to look for another interpretation of the novel. There are just too many questions that the sociological or the Freudian approaches fail to answer. Why do the dwarfs try to steal Paul's typewriter? When it is stolen, why do the girls put it under their skirts? What is that singing bone which tells stories to Snow White? The surrealistic images and episodes which appear on almost every page refuse to be naturalized and seem utterly irrelevant or digressive. How are we supposed to interpret the passages in block letters like the following?

THE REVOLUTION OF THE PAST GENERATION IN THE RELIGIOUS SCIENCES HAS SCARCELY PENETRATED POPULAR CONSCIOUSNESS AND HAS YET TO SIGNIFICANTLY INFLUENCE PUBLIC ATTITUDES THAT REST UPON TOTALLY OUTMODED CONCEPTIONS. (*SW*, p. 54)

This looks like a quotation from the kind of book Barthelme would make fun of, some trivial *objet trouvé*. It is impossible for the reader to know whether or not the narrator adheres to these statements, because there is no comment before or after.

The fifteen questions that conclude the first part of *Snow White* cast some light on the main enigmas of this novel. The narrator, who will never be identified, apparently tries to communicate with his reader:

1. Do you like the story so far? Yes (   ) No (   )

2. Does Snow White resemble the Snow White you remember? Yes (   ) No (   ) (*SW*, p. 82)

Solicitously, he even asks how we would like the story to
develop from that point. But, at the last moment, the question-
naire takes an unexpected turn:

15. In your opinion, should human beings have more
shoulders? (   ) Two sets of shoulders? (   ) Three (   ) (*SW*,
p. 83)

The naïve reader who thought he had at last made contact with
the elusive narrator must feel that someone has been pulling his
leg.[27] The moral of this, of course, is that the narrator is no more
real than the characters in the story; the only palpable object is
the book called *Snow White* in which a number of puppets are
made to perform incredible stunts.

This is not, therefore, a pedagogic or didactic novel, as Lasch
would like us to believe. It is a collection of random sequences
and fragments. Lasch's interpretation is instructive, however:
it shows that the novel's readers feel free to develop any
interpretation they like, since there is no built-in logic (such as a
chronology) to account for the various parts and elements. The
only acceptable statements about this novel, it seems, could
only be tautological. This is, then, a solipsistic novel which
does not create any value and does not leave any residue, be it in
the form of a story or a message. Or, perhaps, it is not a novel at
all. This bourgeois genre has always been felt to be related to
the economic world; it has contributed largely in developing
the kind of cultural consensus necessary to the growth of
modern capitalism. What the critics objected to in *Lolita* was
its slick frivolity – in other words, its economic and didactic
worthlessness. Barthelme has this in common with Nabokov:
he unceremoniously dismisses the hallowed values which, too
often, serve as a cover for petty economic interests.

*

In 'The Balloon', clearly one of his best fictions, Barthelme
shows how fiction can avoid creating a surplus value, a
residue.[28] This appears, at first, as a linear story. The first-
person narrator explains how he put up the balloon over
Manhattan, how the New Yorkers reacted in their attempt to
naturalize the object, how, eventually, the balloon became
integrated in the New York skyscape, and finally how and

why it was removed after the return of the narrator's girlfriend. In the process, the balloon is submitted to various manipulations and deprived of its objecthood. Those who 'write messages on the surface' (*UPUA*, p. 16) seem to use it as a support (like city walls) on which to write or paint. For the children who play on it, it is simply a huge toy which does not *represent* something else; it does not *look like* a landscape with 'small valleys as well as slight knolls or mounds' (*UPUA*, p. 17), it *is* a landscape, just as a broomstick can 'be' a horse. The 'unobjectifying' process begins when a man evolves the notion 'sullied' about it and considers it as 'an imposture, something inferior to the sky that had formerly been there' (*UPUA*, p. 18). As far as this man is concerned, the balloon is a mock sky, a poor substitute for the '*radiant Manhattan sky*' (*UPUA*, p. 18), a second-rate painting, an artefact which emulates reality. This critic, by applying the old Platonic theory that artefacts are necessarily inferior to nature, suddenly becomes blind to the originality of the object, and does not realize that it is more appealing than the grey sky of the megalopolis at that time of year.

In the next paragraph, a new step is taken: the balloon is equated to a given sum of money (which has an exchange value), though it is completely devoid in itself of either exchange or utility value. If it did have such a value, it would be an exaggerated token of gratitude from the employer to his employee for a service that most of us would consider to be a disservice (bruising tulips). Or perhaps it would be a bonus given as an incentive to the employee to produce more value for his employer's benefit. At this point, the balloon as object has completely been forgotten; it has been replaced by the balloon as token or sign. As such, it gets its value from the system of which it is part. Quite logically, it is immediately compared to those transitional objects described by D. W. Winnicott in *Transitional Objects and Transitional Phenomena* (a blanket, a napkin, a toy), which the child uses spontaneously to abandon its oral relation to its mother and achieve a true object relation. No matter how trivial the object is, what is important is that it should be charged with psychic energy (that it should be cathected, in Freudian terms) by the subject. At this point, the balloon has lost its object value to become a symbol. One has the feeling here that Barthelme is illustrating, or making fun of, Peirce's typology of signs.

Evidently Barthelme strongly disapproves of this semiotic inflation which gradually banishes the balloon *qua* object, *qua* 'concrete particular' (a felicitous phrase used earlier in the text), and gradually changes it into what W. K. Wimsatt once called a 'concrete universal', something more, or other, than it apparently is. (Of course, Wimsatt was using this phrase in reference to a literary work as a whole, and not in connection with a particular object or animal created or described within the work itself (Moby Dick, for instance).) It suddenly dawns upon the reader that what is being discussed in this fiction is not the unlikely UFO but rather the fiction itself. The New Yorkers' comments mentioned at the beginning of this chapter ('monstrous pourings', 'Has unity been sacrificed for a sprawling quality?') would naturally fit a text better than an object like the balloon. In the last paragraph, when the narrator discusses the balloon with his girlfriend, he says: 'you asked if it was mine; I said it was. The balloon, I said, is a spontaneous autobiographical disclosure having to do with the unease I felt at your absence, and with sexual deprivation' (*UPUA*, p. 21). The phrase 'spontaneous autobiographical disclosure' would apply much better to the fiction than to the UFO. The narrator seems to be confusing the balloon *qua* object and 'The Balloon' *qua* fiction – which implies that this story is only about itself: its apparition, its form and colour, the comments it elicited from the critics, and so on. At the same time, however, the surrealistic image (somewhat reminiscent of a painting by Magritte) has been strongly impressed on the reader's imagination by this succession of semiotic displacements. We share the narrator's difficulty in distinguishing between the two balloons, and fail to achieve a unified view of our reading experience.

Here Barthelme strains our intelligence and imagination, to leave us in a mental daze, much as Escher does in such works as *Convex and Concave*, or *Cube With Magic Ribbons*, which we cannot possibly view as simultaneously both convex and concave. He virtually prevents us from naturalizing his fictions, urging us, instead, to see them as objects, as solid blocks. We can no longer distinguish between the work – *l'œuvre*, in Roland Barthes's term, what can be held in the hands – and the text – which is held in language[29] – simply because no clear interpretation seems to evolve. Must we do what Borges' Pierre Menard did for *Don Quixote*; must we rewrite the text verbatim, without adding our own comments? Barthelme seems to

71

be coaching his readers into developing a kind of Escherian perception that goes beyond the primitive 'iconic perception' about which Ernst Cassirer wrote. His stance is less anti-intellectual than pro-creative; his ultimate dream, he seems to suggest in 'See the Moon?', is to create the world anew – even if its expression can be no more than the sentence, itself 'a man-made object, not the one we wanted, of course, but still a construction of man, a structure to be treasured for its weakness, as opposed to the strength of stones' ('The Sentence', *CL*, p. 114).

*

Barthelme thus challenges the reader and the critic in a variety of ways which go far beyond pure provocation and raise, as we have tried to show, some fundamental questions about modern literary art. He also provides a surface readability, a 'text of pleasure' which makes it possible to dispense with the fundamental questions: the text can be enjoyed as pure comedy, linguistic slapstick, 'surrealism', 'music', and so on. But, if one tries – as indeed one must in the end – to go for the 'essential', the particular characteristic of Barthelme's fictions remains that they make any single grid of reading or approach seem inadequate: a formalistic and reductive practice superimposed upon the complexity of the sentence or the text. The question with which this study has concerned itself is that of the interpretation of a contemporary text. Some will say that in the last analysis this is a matter of individual taste and talent, with all the multiple meanings open to any response. Should we, then, settle for a pluralistic, eclectic, ecumenical (the metaphors vary) approach: a sort of critical *stereography*? Or, perhaps, for *undecidability*, a recognition of the impossibility of assigning any fixity of meaning to such writing? Both of these attitudes are frequently encountered in contemporary discussion of the growing body of innovative writing. Yet ultimately neither is satisfying.

Michael Riffaterre, in a recent article, sums up the aporias that await alternatives of this kind when he observes: 'Yield to indeterminacy and the text remains an enigma; wave your troubles away and its uniqueness is lost. In both cases interpretation is defeated.'[30] And yet one is tempted to pursue the theme – if only because it is so often prominently and explicitly displayed to us by Barthelme himself. His text is indeed a text of 'unbinding' (A. Green), of the labile nature of self and speech, littered with fragments of (usually) failed attempts at interpretations of all kinds: semiotic, psychological, sociological, and so on. But what must be emphasized here is not so much the self-reflexiveness as the vacillation, the area of play. What Barthelme offers is a bright theatre of meaning; he does not impose closure and continuity where a condition of fracture and carnivalesque disparity obtains. One cannot even be sure that the heterogeneity of the material can be subsumed ('sublated') under a dialectical process (say, 'the dialectical comprehension of ruptures', as Marxist aesthetics would have it). What does emerge with force from all this is a presence, a poise, one might say, *at the brink*.

This may be, as others have argued, a characteristic feature of post-modernism, which situates itself in a (post?-) apocalyptic vision. Such vision has a 'negative' aspect, concerned with 'a minimalist arena of survival', and a more 'positive' one, in which some sort of transcendence and sense is reintroduced, 'starting over, rebuilding from zero, including the reconstruction of language and communication'.[31] Barthelme's stories eschew the teleological implications of the distinction between negative and positive aspects, yet they effectively *stage* this distinction, they hover in this space of uncertainty and vertigo.

Riffaterre's answer to an uncertainty he evidently cannot bear, to the apparent 'ungrammaticality' of a text, is, in fact, an unregenerate defence of semiotics. The case is strongly argued, and our study shows that we would be the last to undervalue the creativity of a semiotic reading of Barthelme's fiction. The key to the triumph of interpretation over undecidability is the passage from a 'linear' to an 'intertextual' reading, which resolves the 'ungrammaticality' originally perceived by the reader in the text. But, in order to effect this shift, Riffaterre has to introduce the existence of an 'intertext', a presupposition to which he gives the name of 'aberrant interpretant'. This is a wonderful invention, worthy of a place, surely, among the many oddities and artefacts of discourse in Barthelme's fictions. In fact, when closely examined, it is seen to have a strong analogy to a celebrated apparatus in contemporary fiction – namely, Maxwell's Demon (a sorting device imagined by the scientist Maxwell, and referred to by Pynchon, which, by separating fast from slow molecules, makes theoretically possible the increase of energy in a system, and thus works against entropy). The aberrant interpretant is a demon, a *diavolo*, a little sorting device whose purpose is to return the teeming anarchy of signs to the order of homeostasis (stability in a system, achieved by counteracting external disturbances) and entropy (or degree of uniformity and stagnation in a system). It is often said that contemporary fiction is entropic, but that is not until it has been sorted out by the demon of interpretation.

It is on this little parable that we should like to conclude our study: a fiction that plays with anarchy, disorder and entropy, yet in the end defeats them and projects an uncanny energy, a constant rejuvenescence; a criticism that is both fascinated and repelled by undecidability and fragmentation, and erects intellectual constructs in order to make sense of it all – until its most serious attempts bring it close to the object of inquiry, so close that they virtually become undistinguishable. Between the violence of interpretation and the suicidal temptation of mimetism, the critical act follows an arduous course. It can't go on, it will go on . . .

NOTES

1 In an interview with Larry McCaffery Barthelme said: 'I really don't have any great enthusiasm for fiction-about-fiction.' After listing the words most commonly used to characterize the current movement in American fiction – post-modernism, metafiction, surfiction, superfiction – he comments: 'I suppose "post-modernism" is the least ugly term' (from McCaffery's transcript).

2 This argument is developed in Maurice Couturier, 'Les Discours du roman', *TREMA*, 2 (October 1977), pp. 19–33.

3 'To seduce entails paying for it by being seduced, that is to say wrested from oneself to become the victim of a spell' (Jean Baudrillard, *De la séduction* (Paris: Galilée, 1980), p. 170; our translation).

4 For example, he writes: 'The difference between signifier and signified intrinsically and implicitly belongs to all that illustrious era spanned by the history of metaphysics; more narrowly and more systematically articulated, it belongs to the narrower era of Christian creationism and infiniticism as they appropriate to themselves the resources of Greek conceptualism' (Jacques Derrida, *De la grammatologie* (Paris: Minuit, 1967), p. 24; our translation).

5 Maurice Blanchot, *L'Entretien infini* (Paris: Gallimard, 1969), p. 451 (our translation). Cf. also Blanchot's latest book, *L'Imagination du désastre* (Paris: Gallimard, 1980), in which he insists on the disruptive, profoundly disturbing, 'disastrous' power of fragmentation, and the 'energy of disappearance' it generates (cf., in particular, pp. 17, 98–101, 118–28).

6 John Leland, 'Remarks Re-Marked, Barthelme: What Curios of Signs!', *Boundary 2*, 5 (Spring 1977), pp. 795–811. But Leland's working theory of fragmentation – 'To fragment presupposes some whole in the first place capable of being fragmented, just as the fragment, incomplete in itself, presupposes a whole or totality which "completes" it' (ibid., p. 795) – is limiting, in precisely the way outlined and criticized by Blanchot. For another example of a superficial view on fragmentation, see J. Hendin in D. Hoffman (ed.), *The Harvard Guide to Contemporary American Writing* (Cambridge, Mass.: Belknap Press of the Harvard University Press, 1979): 'Fragmentation of character and narrative often serve as devices for allaying anxiety' (ibid., p. 241).

7 Gilles Deleuze, *Logique du sens* (Paris: Minuit, 1972).

8 Sigmund Freud, *Jokes and their Relations to the Unconscious* (1905), in *The Standard Edition of the Complete Psychological Works of Sigmund Freud*, trans. and ed. James Strachey (London: Hogarth Press, 1959–74), vol. 8, p. 233.

9 Deleuze, op. cit., pp. 164–5 (our translation).

10 Jacques Lacan, *Écrits* (Paris: Seuil, 1966) (our translation).

11 Concerning the question of allegory in post-modernist aesthetics, we are indebted to a two-part essay by Craig Owens, 'The Allegorical Impulse: Toward a Theory of Postmodernism', *October*, 12 (Spring 1980), pp. 67–86, and 13 (Summer 1980), pp. 59–80. For a further discussion, see the two texts referred to in the essay: Paul de Man, *Allegories of Reading* (New Haven, Conn.: Yale University Press, 1979); and Roland Barthes, *Image Music Text*, trans. S. Heath (New York: Hill & Wang, 1977). For an indication of de Man's theory of allegory in post-modernist texts, here is one of the definitions quoted: 'The paradigm for all texts consists of a figure (or a system of figures) and its deconstruction. But since this model cannot be closed off by a final reading, it engenders, in its turn, a supplementary figural superposition which narrates the unreadability of the prior narration. As distinguished from primary deconstructive narratives centered on figures and ultimately always on metaphor, we can call such narratives to the second (or third) degree allegories. Allegorical narratives tell the story of the failure to read' (op. cit., p. 205).

12 This is a very brief summary of a major question in psychoanalysis. For a more detailed presentation, see in particular J. Laplanche and S. Leclaire, 'The Unconscious: A Psychoanalytic Study', *Yale French Studies*, 48 (1972), and of course Jacques Lacan's *Écrits*. I (RD) have attempted elsewhere to pursue the implications of the 'original' symbolic operation in a literary text: see Régis Durand, ' "The Captive King": The Absent Father in Melville's Text', in R. C. Davis (ed.), *The Fictional Father* (Amherst, Mass.: University of Massachusetts Press, 1981).

13 Sigmund Freud, 'Mourning and Melancholia' (1917), in *A General Selection from the Works of Sigmund Freud*, ed. John Rickman (New York: Doubleday, 1957).

14 For an excellent study of the metapsychological dimension of this novel, see Robert C. David, 'Post-Modern Paternity: Donald Barthelme's *The Dead Father*', *Delta*, 8 (1979), pp. 127–40.

15 See Freud's 'Delusions and Dreams in Jensen's *Gradiva*' (1907), in *The Standard Edition*, vol. 9, pp. 7–95.

16 Jean Baudrillard, in particular, especially in *L'Échange symbolique et la mort* (Paris: Gallimard, 1973), *De la séduction* and *Simulacres et simulations* (Paris: Galilée, 1981). A whole study of the interface between textuality and reality, in particular, could be made with reference to the last book cited.

17 Jerome Klinkowitz, in his 'Postface: 1980' to the second edition of his *Literary Disruptions* (Urbana, Ill.: University of Illinois Press, 1980), notes the affinity of this technique with improvisational jazz, and adds: 'The play of elements, both linguistic and contextual, reminds us that ours is an age of performance' (ibid., p. 210). I (RD) have discussed the performative mode in our culture in two essays: Régis Durand, 'The Disposition of the Voice', in M. Benamou and C. Caramello (eds), *Postmodern Performance* (Madison, Wisc.: Coda Press, 1977), and 'The Anxiety of Performance', *New Literary Theory*, 12 (Fall 1980), pp. 167–76.

18 Vladimir Nabokov, *The Annotated Lolita* (New York: McGraw-Hill, 1970), p. 7.

19 V. Nabokov, *Ada* (New York: McGraw-Hill, 1969), p. 360.

20 See Douglas R. Hofstadter's analysis of this lithograph in *Gödel, Escher, Bach* (New York: Vintage Books, 1980), pp. 714–15.

21 See Vladimir Propp, *Morphologie du conte* (Paris: Seuil, 1965), and A. Greimas, *Sémantique structurale* (Paris: Larousse, 1966).

22 Larry McCaffery's transcript of his interview with Barthelme.

23 Nabokov once said: 'Satire is a lesson, parody is a game' (interview with L. S. Dembo, *Wisconsin Studies in Contemporary Literature*, 8, 2 (Spring 1967), p. 30).

24 The character's name is Dale. The narrator complains that 'he won't focus properly' (Clarence Major, *Reflex and Bone Structure* (New York: Fiction Collective, 1975), p. 100).

25 Roland Barthes once dreamt of an ideal world in which people would use only referentless deictics (*Roland Barthes* (Paris: Seuil, 1975), p. 169). Barthelme seems to have partially fulfilled this dream at times.

26 Christopher Lasch, *The Culture of Narcissism* (New York: Warner Books, 1979), p. 263.

27 Barthelme may be parodying books meant 'to free yourself from self-imposed limits and fulfill your potential', like Arbie M. Dale's *Twenty Minutes a Day to a More Powerful Intelligence* (New York: Playboy Press Paperbacks, 1979), which offers questions like the following: 'For example, you might ask yourself why people have five fingers; or why typewriter paper is usually sized $8\frac{1}{2}'' \times 11''$; or why wheels are round' (ibid., p. 163).

28 I (MC) have analysed this fiction in Maurice Couturier, 'Barthelme's Uppity Bubble: "The Balloon"', *Revue française d'études américaines*, 9 (October 1979), pp. 183–201.

29 Roland Barthes, 'Théorie du texte', *Encyclopedia Universalis*, vol. 15 (1973).

30 Michael Riffaterre, 'Interpretation and Undecidability', *New Literary History*, 12, 2 (Winter 1981), pp. 227–42.

31 Richard Falk, in a note on post-modernism, in *Performing Arts Journal*, 16 (1981).

BIBLIOGRAPHY

WORKS BY DONALD BARTHELME

Novels

Snow White. New York: Atheneum, 1967. London: Cape, 1968.
The Dead Father. New York: Farrar, Straus & Giroux, 1976. London: Routledge & Kegan Paul, 1977.

Collections of stories and short works

Come Back, Dr Caligari. Boston, Mass.: Little, Brown, 1964. London: Eyre & Spottiswoode, 1966.
Unspeakable Practices, Unnatural Acts. New York: Farrar, Straus & Giroux, 1968. London: Cape, 1969.
City Life. New York: Farrar, Straus & Giroux, 1970. London: Cape, 1971.
The Slightly Irregular Fire Engine. New York: Farrar, Straus & Giroux, 1971.
Sadness. New York: Farrar, Straus & Giroux, 1972. London: Cape, 1973.
Guilty Pleasures. New York: Farrar, Straus & Giroux, 1974.
Amateurs. New York: Farrar, Straus & Giroux, 1976. London: Routledge & Kegan Paul, 1977.
Great Days. New York: Farrar, Straus & Giroux, 1979. London: Routledge & Kegan Paul, 1979.

Periodical publications

'The Emerging Figure'. *Forum*, 3 (Summer 1961), pp. 23–4.
'The Case of the Vanishing Product'. *Harper's*, 223 (October 1961), pp. 30–2.
'After Joyce'. *Location*, 1 (Summer 1964), pp. 13–16.
'The Tired Terror of Graham Greene'. *Holiday*, 39 (April 1966), pp. 146, 148–9.
Untitled commentary on 'Paraguay'. In Rust Hills (ed.), *Writer's Choice*, pp. 25–6. New York: David McKay, 1974.
'A Symposium on Fiction' (with William H. Gass, Grace Paley and Walker Percy). *Shenandoah*, 27 (Winter 1976), pp. 3–31.

SELECTED CRITICISM OF DONALD BARTHELME

Aldridge, John W. 'Donald Barthelme and the Doggy Life'. *Atlantic*, 222 (July 1968), pp. 89–91. Reprinted, *The Devil and the Fire*, pp. 216–66. New York: Harper's Magazine Press, 1972.

Bocock, Maclin. '"The Indian Uprising"; or Donald Barthelme's Strange Object Covered with Fur'. *Fiction International*, 4–5 (1975), pp. 134–46.

Couturier, Maurice. 'Barthelme, ou la contamination'. *Delta* (Montpellier, France), 8 (May 1979), pp. 107–26.

—— 'Barthelme's Uppity Bubble: "The Balloon"'. *Revue française d'études américaines*, 9 (October 1979), pp. 183–201.

Critique, 16, 3 (1975). Special Barthelme issue.

Dervin, Daniel A. 'Breast Fantasy in Barthelme, Swift, and Philip Roth: Creativity and Psychoanalytic Structure'. *American Imago*, 33 (1976), pp. 102–22.

Dickstein, Morris. *Gates of Eden: American Culture in the Sixties*, *passim*. New York: Basic Books, 1977.

Durand, Régis. 'L'Erre: déplacements chez Barthelme'. *TREMA* (University of Paris III), 2 (October 1977), pp. 71–80.

Gass, William H. 'The Leading Edge of the Trash Phenomenon'. *New York Review of Books*, 10 (25 April 1968), pp. 5–6. Reprinted in *Fiction and the Figures of Life*, pp. 97–103. New York: Knopf, 1970.

Guerard, Albert J. 'Notes on the Rhetoric of Anti-Realistic Fiction'. *TriQuarterly*, 30 (Spring 1974), pp. 3–30.

Hassan, Ihab. *Paracriticisms*, *passim*. Urbana, Ill.: University of Illinois Press, 1975.

Klinkowitz, Jerome. 'Donald Barthelme'. In *Literary Disruptions*, pp. 62–81, 212–17. Urbana, Ill.: University of Illinois Press, 1975.

—— 'Donald Barthelme'. In *Dictionary of Literary Biography*, vol. 1, pp. 34–9. Detroit, Mich.: Gale Research, 1978.

Leland, John. 'Remarks Re-Marked, Barthelme: What Curios of Signs!'. *Boundary 2*, 5 (Spring 1977), pp. 795–811.

McCaffery, Larry. 'Meaning and Non-Meaning in Barthelme's Fiction'. *Journal of Aesthetic Education*, 13 (January 1979), pp. 69–80.

—— 'Donald Barthelme and the Metafictional Muse'. *Sub-Stance*, 28 (1980), pp. 75–88.

Maloy, Barbara. 'Barthelme's *The Dead Father*: Analysis of an Allegory'. *Linguistics in Literature*, 2, 2 (1977), pp. 43–119.

Rother, James. 'Parafiction: The Adjacent Universe of Barth, Barthelme, Pynchon, and Nabokov'. *Boundary 2*, 5 (Fall 1976), pp. 21–44.

Scholes, Robert. 'Metafiction'. *Iowa Review*, 1 (Fall 1970), pp. 100–15. Reprinted in *Fabulation and Metafiction*. Urbana, Ill.:

University of Illinois Press, 1979.

Stevick, Philip. 'Lies, Fictions, and Mock Facts'. *Western Humanities Review*, 30 (Winter 1973), pp. 332–62.

Stott, William. 'Donald Barthelme and the Death of Fiction'. *Prospects*, 1 (1975), pp. 369–86.

Tanner, Tony. *City of Words, passim.* New York: Harper & Row, 1971.

Weixlemann, Joe and Sher. 'Barth and Barthelme Recycle the Perseus Myth'. *Modern Fiction Studies*, 25 (Summer 1979), pp. 191–207.

Wilde, Alan. 'Barthelme Unfair to Kierkegaard: Some Thoughts on Modern and Postmodern Irony'. *Boundary 2*, 5 (Fall 1976), pp. 45–70.

Focus on undecidability 17

No single meaning —17

No referential anchoring 17

23 — Theme? B ? ... (illegible handwritten notes)

26 Speech is difficult but there are reasons for the difficulty

31 RFH— "a story about epistemological uncertainty" — Contrast about political figure)

EOT: D captures "the cultural unconscious" American — ... Existential suevivint — ... of postcapitalism (44) ... explosion ... 60s stars ... slow death of technological rational society ... (Debord?) ... what victim of ...